Cultural Capital

This book describes the role of *paisanazgo* (a norm emphasizing solidarity between persons from the same locale) among Zapotec urban migrants, especially in regard to mutual aid and the formation of migrant associations. Among these migrants, paisanazgo is not just a passive cultural resource or a matter of "traditional" patterns of mutual aid that have been brought from the provinces and implemented in the city. Rather, norms of solidarity and mutual aid between migrants—along with supporting forms of social organization—constitute a special kind of cultural capital that is actually brought into being as the Zapotec face the challenges of day-to-day life in the city. Zapotec migrants' uses of paisanazgo, however, are not automatic processes, especially in terms of formal migrant associations. As much as they reflect broad value orientations, formal migrant associations are also a continuing response to the course of national development, especially in terms of the Mexican government's attempts to incorporate the hinterlands by extending infrastructure and services. In order to illustrate how and why this is so, this study focuses on three communities of Mountain Zapotec migrants in Mexico City. An examination of these three groups provides the basis for an analysis of ethnic reproduction and innovation among indigenous peasant migrants in Latin American cities.

PROFMEX Series
Michael C. Meyer, General Editor
Oscar J. Martínez, Assistant Editor
James W. Wilkie, Advisory Editor
Clark W. Reynolds, Advisory Editor

PROFMEX
The Consortium of U.S. Research Programs for Mexico

Directors
James W. Wilkie, University of California, Los Angeles, President
John H. Coatsworth, University of Chicago, Chicago
Theo Crevenna, University of New Mexico, Albuquerque
Dale Beck Furnish, Arizona State University, Tempe
Paul Ganster, San Diego State University, San Diego
José Z. García, New Mexico State University, Las Cruces
Richard E. Greenleaf, Tulane University, New Orleans
Ronald G. Hellman, City University of New York, New York
Oscar J. Martínez, University of Arizona, Tucson
Michael C. Meyer, University of Arizona, Tucson
Silvia Ortega Salazar, Universidad Autónoma Metropolitana, Mexico City
Clark W. Reynolds, Stanford University, Stanford
Samuel Schmidt, University of Texas, El Paso
Cathryn Thorup, University of California, San Diego
Leonard Waverman, University of Toronto, Toronto
Sidney Weintraub, University of Texas, Austin

Lane Ryo Hirabayashi

Cultural Capital

Mountain Zapotec Migrant Associations
in Mexico City

The University of Arizona Press
Tucson

The University of Arizona Press
www.uapress.arizona.edu

© 1993 The Arizona Board of Regents
All rights reserved. Published 1993
First paperback edition 2015

Printed in the United States of America
19 18 17 16 15   6 5 4 3 2

ISBN-13: 978-0-8165-1377-2 (cloth)
ISBN-13: 978-0-8165-3170-7 (paper)

Sections of Chapter 6 were first published in an earlier article "On the Formation of Associations in Mexico: Mixtec and Mountain Zapotec Cases" in *Urban Anthropology* 12 (1983): 29–44. Parts of Chapter 2 appeared in an earlier form in "The Migrant Village Association in Latin America: A Comparative Analysis" in the *Latin American Research Review* 21 (1986): 7–29.

Library of Congress Cataloging-in-Publication Data
Hirabayashi, Lane Ryo.
    Cultural capital : Mountain Zapotec migrant associations in Mexico City / Lane Ryo Hirabayashi.
      p. cm. — (PROFMEX series)
    Includes bibliographical references and index.
    ISBN 0-8165-1377-5
    1. Zapotec Indians—Migrations. 2. Rural-urban migration—Mexico—Mexico City. 3. Zapotec Indians—Social conditions. I. Title. II. Title: Paisanazgo, mutual aid, and regional associations among mountain Zapotec migrants in Mexico City. III. Series.
F1221.Z3H57   1993
304.8'08997'6—dc20   92-46230
                                                CIP

∞ This paper meets the requirements of ANSI/NISO Z39.48-1992 (Permanence of Paper).

To my parents
and
To each of my teachers

CONTENTS

List of Figures and Tables	ix
Preface	xi
Acknowledgments	xiii
PART I Migrants and Associations	1
1. Introduction	3
2. Paisanazgo and Migrant Associations	10
PART II Mountain Zapotec Life in the Region and the Capital	25
3. The Rural–Urban Interface	27
4. The Communities of Origin	41
5. Patterns of Out-Migration	63
6. The Regional Bases of Migrant Social Relations	82
PART III Interpretations	109
7. Ethnographic Analysis	111
8. Conclusion	123
REFERENCE MATERIAL	131
Notes	133
Bibliography	141
Index	153

FIGURES AND TABLES

Figure 1.1. The District of Villa Alta and the State of Oaxaca   6

Figure 2.1. Territorial and Administrative Bases of Migrant Associations   15

Table 5.1. Motives for Out-Migration by Theme and Orientation   78

Table 8.1. Characteristics of the Three Communities and Their Out-Migrants   124

PREFACE

The roots of this book go back to 1975, when I spent a summer in a Mountain Zapotec village I will call Ralu'a in the Rincón, an area of the Mexican state of Oaxaca in the rugged Sierra Juárez mountains northeast of Oaxaca City. While gathering data relating to the topic of out-migration, I was impressed by the communal sensibility still evident in the civic affairs of the Mountain Zapotec villages I visited. In Ralu'a, mutual aid constitutes a particularly important part of daily life.

The following summer I conducted another short-term field project focusing on the social organization of Ralu'an migrants in Mexico City. After having lived in Ralu'a, I was fascinated to see that social solidarity, cooperation, and mutual aid were also crucial in the initial adjustment and long-term adaptation of Ralu'an migrants in the capital.

Even more intriguing was the fact that some of the Ralu'an migrants tried to form two regional associations, but neither lasted for very long. By contrast, migrants in Mexico City from the village here referred to as Lahoya, an agricultural community near Ralu'a, had organized a number of village development associations, which were active for the better part of a decade. Trying to account for the formation of migrant associations, as well as determining why they varied in form, focus, and efficacy, presented an ethnographic puzzle that lies at the heart of this book.

Special ties between migrants who are *paisanos,* or "people from the same locale"—including formal migrant associations—are of great interest intellectually and comparatively because the literature in urban studies records their existence among migrants in North and Latin America, Asia, Africa, the Middle East, and the Pacific Islands (see Altamirano and Hirabayashi forthcoming).

Ties between paisanos, including migrant associations, are also of great interest to me personally because of their relevance to my own extended family's experiences in the United States. As an undergraduate I wrote a paper on mutual aid practices in Japan and among Japanese Americans in California and the American West in general. I learned from my father that my paternal grandfather came to America with a group of relatives and friends from Japan immediately prior to the Gentlemen's Agreement of 1908. Both when he was single and after he married my grandmother, who was also from his village, "same place" ties among their fellow migrants were central in adapting to life and labor in the state of Washington (see Miyabara 1988).

A few years after completing my doctoral dissertation, I also learned that the *bygdelag,* or regional, movement played an important role in the Norwegian immigrant community in America in the early twentieth century (Lovoll 1975). Although I have yet to establish proof of direct involvement, my maternal great-grandparents came from Norway and lived in both the Pacific Northwest and the Midwest, areas in the United States where the bygdelag movement flourished.

What is more, my wife's extended family participates in a number of associations in the Philippines and in the United States which are regional in nature. Some of these associations, like the Santo Niño de Cebu, have affiliates in California whose functions we have attended over the years.

In short, my intellectual interests, family history, and personal background have all informed this study of Zapotec migrant associations. In turn, the Zapotec's cooperation with my project has given me an understanding not only of Mountain Zapotec migrant communities in Mexico City but also insights into how my Japanese, Norwegian, and Filipino relatives drew on regional ties in their search for community in the United States.

ACKNOWLEDGMENTS

While the thoughts expressed in this book are solely my responsibility, I would like to acknowledge collectively, first and foremost, literally hundreds of Zapotec who talked to me in Oaxaca, Mexico City, and Los Angeles. Although it might surprise them, given the years and distance that now separate us, our time together had a profound and lasting effect on my academic career.

I owe special thanks to Professor Laura Nader of the Department of Anthropology at the University of California at Berkeley, for introducing me to the literature on the Zapotec of Oaxaca and for suggesting that I study Mountain Zapotecs in Mexico City. She also facilitated my work by helping me to obtain research grants and by providing many contacts in the Rincón and in Mexico City. Similarly, I am grateful to Professor Nelson H. H. Graburn, who spent countless hours in discussions with me, sharing his encyclopedic knowledge of anthropology as well as his enthusiasm for the field.

Professors George M. Foster, Woodrow W. Borah, and Janice E. Perlman have also given me the benefit of their instruction, guidance, and support. Each conveyed much to me about the craftsmanship involved in research.

Three different institutions helped me prepare for and carry out my fieldwork. At the University of California at Berkeley, the Department of Anthropology and the Center for Latin American Studies provided training and funding that sustained my research and studies. Additional funding came from the Inter-American Foundation, which awarded me a generous grant to pursue fieldwork for two continuous years from 1977 to 1979. I also appreciate the foundation's flexibility, which included complete intellectual freedom as my research topic evolved. As a condition for holding their graduate fellowship, the foundation required an affiliation with a Mexican university. I am grateful to the Colegio de México in Mexico City for initially sponsoring my fieldwork, and to Dr. Roberto Salazar, then of the colegio's Centro de Estudios Sociológicos, who supervised the affiliation.

Drs. Fernando Cámera Barbachano, Claude S. Fischer, Fadwa El Guindi, Robert Van Kemper, Philip C. Parnell, Gobi Stromberg, and Kate Young gave me valuable advice and direction in the early stages of my fieldwork. At various points during my research in Mexico, I also had the privilege of discussions with Drs. Lourdes Arizpe, Nancy Modiano, Humberto Muñoz, Claudio Stern, Stefano Varese, and Sra. Lini de Vries. Each offered important suggestions based on their experience and expertise.

Licenciado Gabriel Brun Martínez and Dr. Larissa Adler de Lomnitz were especially hospitable during my extended fieldwork stay in Mexico City. Cordial discussions with each about anthropology and research in Mexico provided many insights, as well as a much appreciated sense of intellectual community.

In the years that have elapsed between the completion of my graduate studies in 1981 and the revision of the present manuscript (carried out intermittently between 1986 and 1992), Professor Teófilo Altamirano has been a major influence on my work. Professors Michael Kearney, Bryan Roberts, and Susan Buck Sutton have also contributed to the formation of the perspective presented here. Professor Evelyn Hu-DeHart gave me encouragement and advice that brought my seemingly never-ending project to a close. Leah Florence provided valuable editorial suggestions early on, and I am very grateful to Alan M. Schroder of the University of Arizona Press, whose editorial acumen sharpened the final version.

Finally, I have been fortunate in receiving support from the Center for Studies of Ethnicity and Race in America, and the Implementation of Multicultural Perspectives and Approaches to Research and Teaching (IMPART) program, both at the University of Colorado at Boulder, that enabled me to prepare the study presented here.

PART I

Migrants and Associations

CHAPTER 1

Introduction

This book describes how Mountain Zapotec migrants employ *paisanazgo*, which prescribes solidarity among "fellow countrymen" from the same locale, in order to effect cooperation and mutual aid among their compatriots in Mexico City. Paisanazgo, as I indicate below, is basically an aspect of culture that social scientists call a norm. Paisanazgo thus encompasses explicit obligations that, in this case, also configure mutual aid, exchange, and association.

Paisanazgo is central to understanding relationships among Mountain Zapotec migrants in Mexico City. What I argue here, though, is that paisanazgo in the urban setting is not just a kind of passive cultural resource equivalent to "traditional" patterns of mutual aid that Zapotecs practice in the provinces. Rather, paisanazgo is a kind of 'cultural capital' that is actually created by urban Zapotecs as they face the day-to-day challenges of city life and of the larger Mexican society of the mid to late twentieth century.[1]

Specifically, I propose that paisanazgo can be thought of as an "embodied" form of cultural capital. Mountain Zapotec migrants have drawn from their heritage and customs in a creative yet systematic fashion in order to effect their cultural and social recomposition in Mexico City. In addition, I argue that, among Mountain Zapotec, certain manifestations of paisanazgo have been energized and shaped by the course of national development, especially as it affected the Sierra Juárez—the region of origin of these Zapotec migrants—between the 1950s and the 1980s. Migrant associations in particular have their basis in the Mountain Zapotec worldview and values, including paisanazgo, but are simultaneously affected by macro-level processes operating at the regional, state, and national levels.

In order to illustrate how and why this is so, this study focuses on three communities of the Mountain Zapotec that manifest differing degrees of Zapotec ethnicity, social solidarity, economic and occupational pursuits, and sociopolitical articulation with the nation. But first, a quick overview of basic concepts and issues—including a discussion of the Mountain Zapotec and of the significance of regionalism in Latin America—will help to frame the theoretical and empirical chapters that follow.

THE ZAPOTEC AND THE MOUNTAIN ZAPOTEC

In 1990 there were an estimated 506,251 monolingual or bilingual speakers of Zapotec in Mexico (Avellaneda Díaz 1990). Since the Zapotec are by no means homogeneous, language stock is the clearest basis by which they can be identified as a group. Utilizing the broad criterion of language, the Zapotec constitute the largest indigenous population in the Mexican state of Oaxaca and the third largest in the country (Muntzel and Pérez González 1987:577).

Although the Zapotec can thus be considered an ethnic population sharing a common geographic area and attributes, including language, there are at least three reasons why they are not regarded as constituting an ethnic group per se. First and most important, the Zapotec lack an overarching political organization apart from that imposed by the nation and the state of Oaxaca. Second, although they share common historical roots, the various Zapotec languages are often mutually unintelligible—a fact that again leads to division rather than unity among the Zapotec as a whole. Third, the Zapotec do not generally share a larger sense of ethnic identity as a people. As a result, experts find it convenient to distinguish several subgroups among the Zapotec of Oaxaca based on language, sociocultural patterns, and settlement in distinct ecological zones. These subgroups include the Zapotec in Oaxaca's central valley, the mountainous north, the southern mountains from the Sierra Miahuatlán to the Pacific coast, and the isthmus (Nader 1969).[2] In short, the complexity of the state and its indigenous peoples should always be kept in mind, and generalizations about the Mountain Zapotec should not necessarily be taken to hold for the Zapotec as a whole or for Mexican indigenous peoples in other settings.

In this book, my focus is on Mountain Zapotec communities and outmigrants to Mexico City. The Mountain Zapotec live in the northern part of the state of Oaxaca, primarily in the district of Villa Alta, an administrative unit made up of twenty-five municipalities (Instituto Nacional de Estadística Geografía e Informática [hereafter INEGI] 1984).[3]

REGIONALISM AND THE SOCIAL ORGANIZATION OF MOUNTAIN ZAPOTEC MIGRANTS

As with other peasants in Latin America who have roots in highland indigenous cultures, the social organization of Mountain Zapotec migrants is far from uniform even though they often share common characteristics both at home and in the capital. For example, when they have sufficient numbers, Mountain Zapotec migrants generally form village or regional associations, though elements like the organizations' foci or goals, organizational forms, and efficacy often vary.

My approach to understanding such variation is primarily ethnographic and is based on a comparative, regionally framed analysis of three groups of Mountain Zapotec migrants in Mexico City. Their communities of origin are located in the Sierra Juárez in the district of Villa Alta northeast of Oaxaca de Juárez (called Oaxaca City here; see Fig. 1.1). All are within four or five hours' walking-distance of each other.

At first glance, the migrant groups in Mexico City from these three provincial communities appear to be similar in a number of important respects. First, migrants from all three towns arrived in the capital in significant numbers between 1960 and 1980. Second, during the same period, migrants were able to adjust to life in the capital relatively quickly, in no small part because they arrived via a process of chain migration, in which earlier migrants, who usually came as single men and women and who had established themselves at great cost, facilitated more recent migrants, who sometimes arrived as entire families. Third, on the basis of paisanazgo, both old and new migrants engaged in mutual aid practices in order to help each other to survive and compete in the new urban setting. Fourth, in each case regional ties and commitments became politicized as migrants formed village, regional, or multidistrict associations in Mexico City.

Despite such similarities, major variations among the three groups of migrants are also apparent. Migrants from the agricultural village of Lahoya in Mexico City between 1960 and the mid-1970s, for example, were characterized by their commitment to highly active village associations, whose primary aim was the development of Lahoya. Two village associations in particular were central to the social organization of Lahoyan migrants in Mexico City. Over time, these associations also became the basis for intense and prolonged factionalism, which eventually divided both the migrants and the residents of the home village. The interesting point here is that the Lahoyans do not

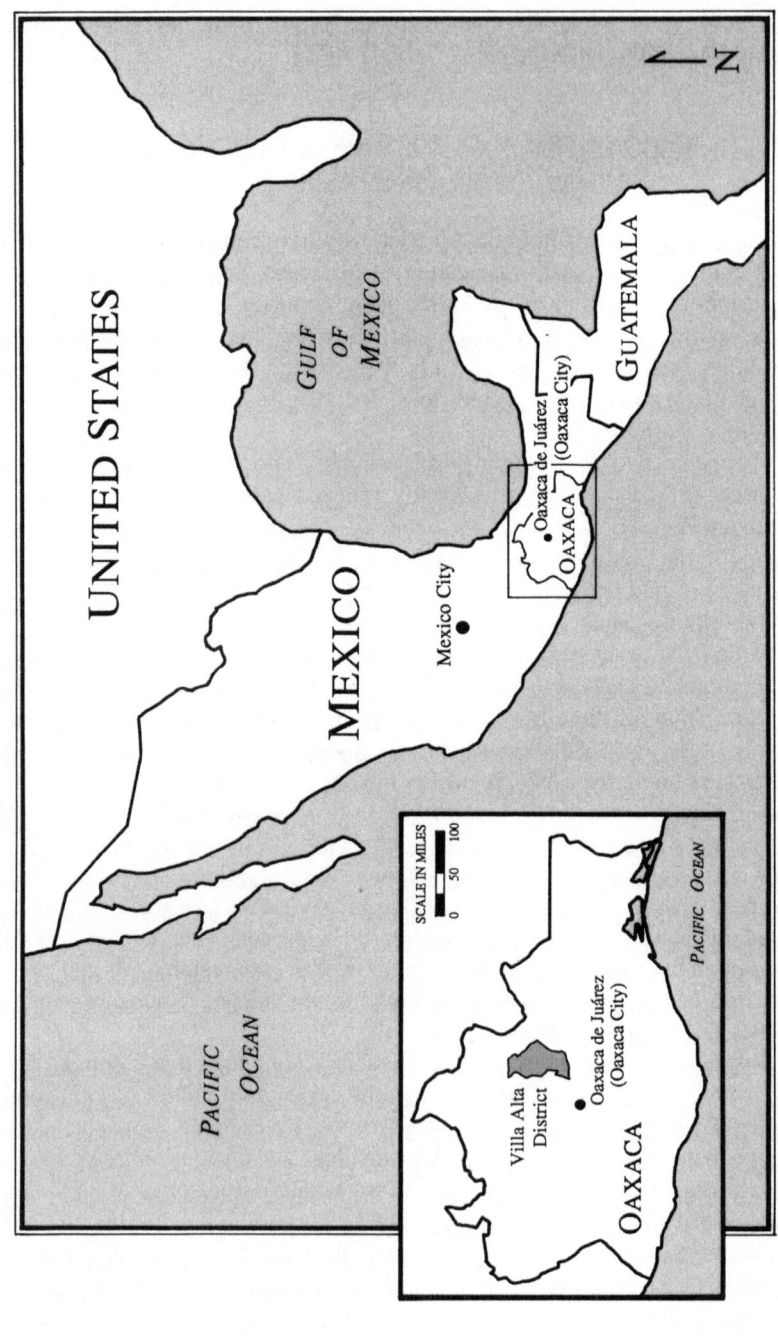

Figure 1.1. The District of Villa Alta and the State of Oaxaca

emphasize mutual aid or cooperative practices either culturally or in the routine of everyday village life.

Two questions can be posed about the Lahoyan case study. First, why is it that the social organization of the Lahoyan migrants in Mexico City revolved so heavily around the formation and activities of village associations, which are predicated, after all, on norms of cooperation and mutual aid? Second, why did factionalism develop among these migrants, and grow to such bitter and overwhelming proportions?

Since the late 1950s, the migration and urban adaptation of migrants from the regional marketing center of Ralu'a have been characterized by informal patterns of mutual aid, although not to the same extent as relations back in the Sierra Juárez, where a plethora of both informal and formal groups permeates community life. Information and services given to new migrants and shared as an integral part of continuing reciprocity networks[4] have been important in enabling Ralu'ans to adjust rapidly to occupational and educational challenges in Mexico City.

Ralu'an migrants retain strong emotional ties to their home village and have been involved in numerous village development projects over the past three decades, but, surprisingly, they have never formed a village-level association. Instead, some of the Ralu'an migrants have been instrumental in the formation of regional-level migrant associations in Mexico City. In fact, two such associations were formed, one in the early 1960s and one toward the end of that same decade. Both were short-lived.

These data suggest the following two comparative questions. First, why was the regional level—which was naturally based on a broader sense of Zapotec identity—emphasized by this group of migrants? Second, why were informal networks more common and effective, especially compared to the Ralu'an regional associations, which were both temporally and materially limited, at least during the period under consideration?

A third community, Villa Alta, is generally regarded as a Spanish-influenced *mestizo* town whose administrative and commercial functions set it apart from the Zapotec villages surrounding it. Although I lack extensive data on Villa Alta that would make my analysis of it fully comparable to the other cases, a recent study by the anthropologist Philip C. Parnell (1988) makes it clear that in the town, as well as in Oaxaca City and Mexico City, Villaltecos have established not one but a number of formal and informal committees and associations. In the urban settings, according to Parnell, the majority of groups within the migrant community tie the organizations to the customs, politics, and development projects of the town.

Considering the latter as a point of comparison with the two more extensively documented cases, one might ask why Villalteco urban migrants seem to carry on rural traditions and even form associations that revolve around the town, just like migrants from neighboring villages that are composed primarily of Zapotec-speaking peasants? Concomitantly, given that they have held a leadership position as the district seat for more than four hundred years, why have the urban Villaltecos not been central in the organization of regional-level migrant activities or associations?[5]

Because the out-migrants to Mexico City from these three communities exhibit both major similarities and interesting and somewhat surprising differences—especially concerning the focus and efficacy of each group's associations—they provide a significant explanatory challenge.

A CONCEPTUAL OVERVIEW

I propose that an analysis of the above questions can benefit from a comparative examination of empirical case studies that are regionally framed. Case studies, however, must be placed within an historical-structural context of internal migration that gives center stage to the complex linkages that tie regions and points of origin to the larger Mexican nation.

Historical structuralism, as I understand it, is a macro-level analysis.[6] An historical-structural perspective on internal migration is based essentially on the following theoretical assumptions. To begin with, the rural and urban spheres must be treated as linked parts in a global whole—in this case, the Mexican nation—which is simultaneously being affected by change, especially in the form of dependent development and the uneven nature of Mexico's industrialization. Concomitantly, internal migration is an integral part of larger processes of uneven development and can only be understood as such. As a result, particular regional and local processes of migration and urban adaptation must be placed within a larger macro-level framework in order to be fully and meaningfully analyzed.

Specifically, my thesis is that the associations formed by Mountain Zapotec migrants in Mexico City during the 1960s and 1970s were rooted in the normative imperatives of paisanazgo but also responded to the Mexican government's programs of rural extension and modernization as these affected the Sierra Juárez generally and the central portion of the district of Villa Alta in particular.[7] This was not, however, a mechanical process; variation had a great deal to do with the political dynamics linking villagers and out-migrants to the Mexican government's modernization programs.

Chapter 2 provides an overview of analytical approaches to migrant social organization in Latin America based on "common origin." To facilitate this objective, and to clarify positions and polemics, I define the terms *pueblismo, paisano, paisanazgo,* and *migrant association.* I also delineate three basic approaches to the study of migrant associations: (1) an approach that is largely sociopsychological and that emphasizes the cultural transitions faced by migrants; (2) one that focuses on migrants' attempts to gain access to scarce resources; and (3) one that is structuralist insofar as migrant associations are seen as migrants' response to regional inequities represented by conditions at the point of origin. Each of these perspectives has demonstrable strengths and weaknesses depending on the analytical task at hand, and each has generated important hypotheses, which are reviewed below.

In order to explore these perspectives and hypotheses further, Part 2 presents the Mountain Zapotec case studies, including information about the points of origin, the processes of out-migration, and the patterns of migrant social organization in Mexico City.

Part 3 explains the thesis linking variations among Zapotec migrant associations to the course of national development. The resulting analysis is of value precisely because such variation is neither fully predicted in the literature nor fully explained by it. Part 3 also explains how and why paisanazgo may be seen as a kind of cultural capital, even though Mountain Zapotec migrants are far from the elite that Bourdieu and others have generally focused upon in this regard (see Lamont and Lareau 1987).

The ethnographic data presented here are important in their own right because they constitute the first book-length study to focus on Zapotec migrants in an urban setting. Beyond this, my aim is to demonstrate that detailed analysis of ethnographic case studies is a productive approach to the issues raised by the creation and persistence of local, territorially based frames of reference in migrant identity and social organization. In this sense, specific case studies can be used to develop *general* insights that inform research on migrant social organization in Mexico, Latin America in general, and beyond. As such, this book reflects both the ethnographic and the comparative orientations that have long been the hallmark of anthropological research.

CHAPTER 2

Paisanazgo and Migrant Associations

Migrant associations in Mexican urban settings are typically based on identification with a home community (*pueblismo*), as well the expectation among migrants that special ties and obligations exist between *paisanos*—that is, compatriots who come from the same locale and who share a common background.

In practice, the intensity of and commitment among migrants to such ideas may vary from weak to strong. In the former instance, an established migrant may feel obligated only to welcome or provide short-term advice or help to a new migrant, especially if there is a substantial gap between their socioeconomic statuses. Only in its strongest manifestations would one expect to see migrants willing and able to organize a formal association based on the norm of solidarity among compatriots.

In order to set the stage for the case studies and analysis that follow, this chapter will review the concepts of paisano, paisanazgo, pueblismo, and migrant association in some detail, exploring possible reasons for variations in the presence, form, and intensity of the migrant association.

PAISANOS, PAISANAZGO, AND PUEBLISMO

While present in the rural setting in Mexico, the notion of special ties among paisanos is especially important and explicit among indigenous peasant migrants in cities. The term *paisano* literally means "fellow countryman" or "compatriot," although a paisano could be from either the same community, region, state, or even nation, depending on the context and situational variables.[1]

I was exposed to the term early in my fieldwork because I often heard Mountain Zapotec migrants refer to each other collectively as paisanos, or sometimes lightly and humorously as *mi paisa,* (a contracted form of *mi paisano*). Upon inquiry I was told that Mountain Zapotec in Mexico City have special ties and obligations to each other because they come from the same village or region. Especially when outside of the village, Ralu'an outmigrants told me, paisanos must demonstrate solidarity in the new, somewhat unfamiliar, and sometimes dangerous environment of the city. In essence, paisanazgo is a norm. Homans defined a norm as "an idea in the minds of the members of a group, an idea that can be put in the form of a specific statement specifying what the members or other[s] . . . should do, ought to do, are expected to do, under given circumstances" (Homans 1950:123). According to Homans's subsequent discussion, a norm is collectively held, is conscious, can be articulated, and involves ideas about expected behavior, all of which are appropriate characterizations of paisanazgo.[2]

Having spent time in the Sierra Juárez, I was aware that the concept of the paisano, and by extension the norm of paisanazgo—or the general principle of loyalty and solidarity among fellow migrants from the same place— reflected local conceptions of identity and affiliation back in Oaxaca. Specifically, in contemporary Mountain Zapotec communities, one's hometown or natal village is often the focal point of identity beyond one's kith and kin, as Nader and others who have done fieldwork in the region have observed (Nader 1969:349). Berg refers to this tendency as *pueblismo,* which he glosses as an ethnocentric orientation revolving around and giving priority to one's community of origin (Berg 1974:25). As people emphasized to Berg in the Mountain Zapotec marketing town of Zoogocho, "Somos Zoogochenses" (We are Zoogochenses). Berg comments that this sentiment was so strong in the 1970s that even residents who were economically much better off than the rest of the members of the community continued to portray themselves as poor, hardworking, indigenous peasants just like everyone else.

The origins of the attitude of pueblismo are unclear, encompassing as they do both pre- and postconquest cultural orientations, the political and administrative organization imposed by the Spaniards, historical trajectories, and competition for local resources such as land. Regarding its preconquest roots, Chance informs us that, compared to cultures in the Valley of Oaxaca or among the Mixteca, social stratification was much less pronounced in the Sierra Zapoteca. In addition, "[t]he customary Mesoamerican settlement pattern of head town . . . with subject hamlets . . . was not as developed. . . . The pattern of small, relatively independent villages intensified during the colonial period" (Chance 1989:13). Chance notes that, apart from local uprisings (one in 1570 and another in 1700), "episodes of any kind that united people on a supra-communal regional or ethnic basis were few and not well organized" (1989:124). He concludes:

> In general, my findings in the Villa Alta jurisdiction support William Taylor's contention that the landholding village—the pueblo—gained importance in the colonial period at the expense of ethnic and regional ties. . . . De la Fuente's ethnographic observation that the most important unit of identification is the pueblo applies equally well to colonial times as it does to the modern scene. (Chance 1989:124)

It is of great interest that the attitude of pueblismo is also a marked characteristic of Spanish peasant culture (Pitt-Rivers 1961:30–31), and the similarities to localism in the Sierra Juárez are striking. Foster notes that

> membership in the local community—the pueblo—stems from birth, and endows the individual with characteristics and prerogatives which time and the process of law cannot erase. . . . This Spanish identification with community of birth reflects an ancient Circum-Mediterranean trait, now dignified in anthropological terminology by the Italian word *campanilismo,* the feeling that one's real world extends only within earshot and sight of the village campanile. (Foster 1960:34–35)

In short, "[t]he Spaniard's sense of attachment to his community is intense," and moreover, "whether one's native town be large or small, the same attachment to, love of, and fierce pride in it are found in each heart" (Foster 1960:34–35). Although Foster acknowledges that antagonisms may divide a given community and that villagers recognize broader links to neighbors, "[a]t the same time against the world there is unity in local patriotism, and a genuinely strong belief that one's community is superior to all others" (1960:34–35).

While the Mountain Zapotec in the sierra did not use it in their everyday conversation, the Spanish phrase *patria chica* effectively captures the magnitude of local identity and commitment to one's natal village, since it literally means "little homeland." Concomitantly, as in Spain, those who feel strong pride in their hometown or village in the sierra frequently express ambivalence, if not outright antipathy, toward neighboring communities that may be less than an hour's walk away.[3] Although I am unable to ascertain the direct influence of Spanish cultural orientations in this regard upon Latin American peasantry, the parallels are striking.

Such attitudes were certainly the case among the denizens of Ralu'a, the town in the Sierra Juárez where I spent the most time. Ralu'ans freely acknowledged that they were Rinconeros—that is, Zapotecs of the geographic area within Villa Alta called the Rincón, or corner—and as such, members of the twelve communities in this area whose residents speak Nexitzo, a language of the Zapotec family. Occasionally, individuals would also acknowledge that they were Zapotec, but I heard this invocation only infrequently, and then usually to indicate a broad genealogical link with President Benito Juárez, the first and only Mexican president of Zapotec descent. First and foremost they saw themselves as Ralu'ans. All of these facts are pertinent in explaining why I consider the concept of paisanazgo the salient principle behind Mountain Zapotec migrant social relations in Mexico City from the 1950s through the 1980s, although I recognize the relevance of concepts like race and ethnicity.

For the Mountain Zapotec, race *is* an operant variable in both the provinces and the city. In this regard, however, it must be remembered that Spaniards reached the sierra very quickly after the fall of Tenochtitlán in 1521. By 1526 they were active in the sierra, and by then they had founded their own administrative town and center, San Ildefonso Villa Alta. Today, the Mountain Zapotec exhibit a full range of phenotypes from the "classic"-looking Zapotecs of San Juan Juquila Vijanos, to the tall, light-skinned, blue- and green-eyed men of Tanetze, who are clearly of mestizo, or mixed Spanish-Indian, descent. Given such circumstances, race operates selectively and situationally and becomes salient when triggered in certain contexts. In addition, it is sometimes difficult in Latin American social settings to draw a clear distinction between racial and socioeconomic prejudice.

I employ the concept of paisanazgo to analyze Mountain Zapotec migrant social relations in Mexico City in preference to that of ethnicity for similar reasons. Ethnicity generally refers to a sense of peoplehood. According to Milton M. Gordon's classic definition, ethnicity can be based on a range of attributes, including race, nationality, or religion (Gordon 1964). In essence, although they recognize that they are Zapotecs (as well as Catholics and Mexicans), this is not generally highlighted in the Mountain Zapotec's self-representations—at least not to outsiders like myself. Rather, individuals stress their roots in a specific village or town of origin, and while they recognize and will acknowledge other dimensions of their identity and heritage if questioned, these are implicit by comparison.[4]

In short, various manifestations of pueblismo were apparent in the communities I visited or read about in the sierra, and people simply refer to themselves as being natives of a particular community in preference to other identities or affiliations. Paisanazgo, it should be re-emphasized, was *not* a concept that I heard people articulate in the communities of the Sierra Juárez. Rather, paisanazgo among Mountain Zapotecs in Mexico City is based on regional frames of identity (like pueblismo) found throughout the Sierra Juárez from the colonial period through the 1980s (de la Fuente [1949] 1977:210; Chance 1989; cf. Butterworth 1975; Romer 1982:155). In other words, preexisting regional sentiments typified by the phenomenon of pueblismo are shaped, re-created, and explicitly articulated in terms of the norm of paisanazgo by Mountain Zapotec migrants in the *urban* setting.[5]

DEFINING MIGRANT ASSOCIATIONS

If paisanazgo provides a norm justifying assistance and mutual aid between dyadic sets of individual migrants and families in an urban setting, it also provides the rationale for collective strategies of adaptation. Thus, paisanazgo underlies formal urban migrant associations, which, depending on their level of organization, are sometimes also called village, regional, or provincial associations.

At whatever level it is formed, a migrant association along these lines is an urban association that is usually voluntary, given that, in Pickvance's words, a "*voluntary association* is a non-statutory, non-commercial organization which is not an institution, which has a formal structure, . . . and where membership is open to any person within the eligible social category" (Pickvance 1986:235).[6] A migrant association is generally formed in an urban setting by out-migrants from a community, region, or in some cases a state for the purpose of both conviviality and mutual aid. It thus provides both moral and tangible resources for individual and collective adaptation to an urban setting. Generally, migrant associations evolve out of informal networks of migrants who are already linked together by ties of kinship, friendship, and propinquity. In contrast to informal social networks, however, migrant associations typically involve a semblance of formal structure such as an organizational name, a charter, by-laws, and sometimes a dues schedule.[7] What distinguishes migrant associations from both voluntary associations in general and ethnic associations per se is that, by definition, migrant associations are based on ties having to do with "common origin" over and above other possible statuses or qualities.[8]

The definition of regional bases underlying "common origin" merits attention in that the concept is variable. Although the geographic territory upon which regionalism is based might appear to be straightforward, it is necessarily subject to definition. The village, the region (however defined), or the larger encompassing district are the parameters most often selected by migrants in Latin America (see Fig. 2.1). As the figure suggests, if numbers and other conditions are favorable, organizations are likely to be based on the most primary and immediate ties, characterized by face-to-face interaction on a daily basis.[9] In any given case, the level selected has to do with the cultural, territorial, and political commitments that migrants have toward their "home" and their "compatriots," however they choose to define them. Similarly, a given member's commitment to a migrant association can vary at the personal

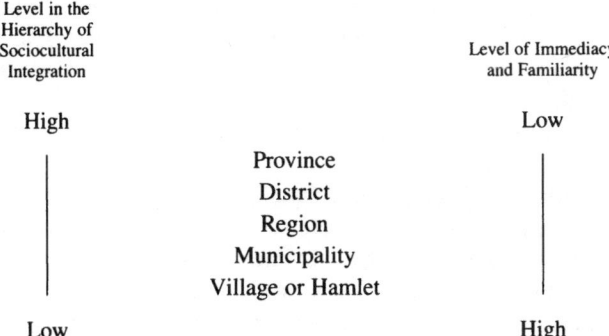

Figure 2.1 Examples of the Territorial and Administrative Bases of Migrant Associations in Latin America

level or over time, ranging from being an organizer or officer to an active participant or a more passive "affiliate."

This said, let us explore three perspectives on why migrants form migrant associations, as well as some of the basic functions that migrant associations are said to serve.

THREE APPROACHES TO MIGRANT ASSOCIATIONS

Like other voluntary associations, migrant associations can have many explicit functions, either singly or in combination. The following three perspectives, advanced in conjunction with empirical research in Mexico and Peru—two sites in Latin America that have received special attention in this regard—explain some of the reasons why migrants form their own associations in urban settings.

Sociopsychological Views

Having probable ties to "modernization theory" (Perlman 1976:91–131), the sociopsychological view asserts that migrant associations help the individual migrant adapt to a new and unfamiliar environment. From this viewpoint, associations form and persist precisely because they help the migrant to bridge the cultural and social gap between the rural and urban settings.

Specific descriptions based on this idea sometimes depict associations as organized around, and primarily dedicated to, convivial and leisure activities in the city. Groups devoted to athletics or to the social or cultural pursuits of their members are examples of this tendency (e.g., Altamirano 1984a:128, 138). Similarly, whatever the activity, associational contact with compatriots in the city is thought to provide a sense of identity, a "psychological anchor," as well as a "medium of sociability and recreation" (Goode 1970:153). Thus, researchers comment that regional associations help to offset the culture shock and alienation new migrants would otherwise be likely to experience if they were totally on their own in, or dispersed throughout, the urban setting. Concomitantly, a sociopsychological view often highlights the fact that new migrants undergo socialization to the city and city ways in migrant associations, informally via conversations and stories or more formally through explicit guidance and/or counseling offered by more experienced compatriots.

Another dimension of the sociopsychological perspective involves the claim that associations can play important regulatory roles among their members. At either a formal or informal level, and for either two or more persons, migrant associations can offer a means of resolving intragroup disputes and conflicts. This is important because, from the migrants' point of view, the urban legal system is relatively unpredictable, not to mention expensive. Their reservations about the urban legal system are further heightened when migrants come from locales where the ideal and the actual pursuit of justice can take a very different form than in the city.

William Mangin's early research on regional associations in Lima, Peru, typifies the combination of rural and urban dimensions of the sociopsychological perspective (e.g., Mangin 1959, 1970a, 1970b; cf. Lewis 1952). A pioneer in the study of migrant associations in Peru, Mangin identified rural cooperative traditions, as well as the maintenance of ties to the home village or region, among the rural migrants he studied in Lima. Mangin also stressed the adaptive functions migrant associations fulfill in helping newcomers to adjust and survive, culturally and socially, in the city.

From a sociopsychological perspective, then, a regional association—whatever its explicit aims—can play a very positive role in helping people to adapt to the urban environment. In the comparatively nonthreatening setting of a regional association, migrants can profit from the experience of more-established peers, who can best mediate and interpret urban life to newcomers. Simultaneously, migrant associations bridge the cultural and social gaps between the points of origin and destination. In this sense, associations address the deep personal needs of migrants, needs that cannot be fully met within the context of other formal or informal urban institutions. In either sense, migrant associations provide a natural medium for the preservation and the reinterpretation of local culture and customs in the city.

Resource-Competition Views

A second broad perspective on regional associations highlights issues of resource competition between migrants and other urban dwellers (see Cohen 1969 and Depres 1975, two key authors from whom this view is generally derived). This perspective requires a model of social stratification in which migrants are portrayed as a distinct group or stratum competing for limited resources within the urban setting. In this context, migrant regional associations may be seen as an explicit strategy to gain enough influence or political power to win access to scarce resources. In this sense, a resource-competition perspective presents a view of migrants as a class in itself and for itself, self-consciously trying to mitigate the unequal basis on which many migrants from the provinces have to compete.

At one level of resource competition, regional associations function as benevolent societies for their members. Associations, that is, provide a tangible mechanism for sharing information about jobs and housing, as well as for giving or receiving psychological, social, and monetary aid during crises. As Roberts (1990) has pointed out, mutual aid along these lines provides very real economic benefits to migrants who would not otherwise be able to afford to pay for or hire such services.

At another level, although their original purposes or manifest functions may not suggest it, regional associations sometimes facilitate the pursuit of economic interests (including establishing certain kinds of businesses or even trade monopolies), and the political interests and goals of their members in the city. These functions appear to be especially heightened in national settings in which social perceptions of race or ethnicity play a role in blocking access to, or the fair distribution of, key resources like jobs, housing, and education. A quick review of three researchers who have used the resource-competition approach in their work will serve to clarify the above points, as well as related issues.

A number of researchers argue that regional associations tend to arise among poor indigenous migrants who come from villages with a strong tradition of cooperation and whose dire circumstances generate a need to act collectively in the city. Claude Bataillon, for example, states in a number of works that communal strategies of urban adaptation arise only among Mexican migrants whose lifestyles are characterized by a persistent indigenous heritage and customs (e.g., Bataillon 1972:163). He also states that communal strategies of adaptation are not carried out at the level of the migrant group as a whole but are the recourse of a small, disadvantaged segment of the group. This segment unites in order to defend itself by clustering in certain occupations and providing mutual aid and support, thus bettering the situation of the group (1972:164).[10] By implication, those migrants with stable jobs and a steady income have much less need or desire to maintain traditional obligations or to become involved in an association. Bataillon's explanation thus involves both ethnic and class-based dimensions of stratification and resource competition.

Carlos Orellana S. (1973) also proposes that village and regional associations are formed solely by Indian migrants who have experienced a strong communal tradition in their point of origin, but beyond this, Orellana posits that certain urban conditions lead to a politicizing experience that transforms migrants' informal networks into formal village or regional associations. In his fieldwork, which focused on Mixtec migrants in Mexico City, Orellana found that informal networks based on kinship or friendship, mutual aid, and propinquity became formalized in urban struggles to obtain a territorial base for Mixtec housing as well as an ethnic territorial enclave. These Mixtec migrants evidently desired to form an organization because through it they could effectively aid each other in an urban setting in which social services were nonexistent, especially in finding temporary lodging and more permanent housing, and obtaining a job. Thus, informal networks, and afterward a formal association, enabled them to maximize control over scarce resources in the city and provided a modicum of competitive advantage in a situation in which they had comparatively little education and few urban job skills.[11] Orellana emphasizes that the Mixtec association in Mexico City provided the basis for Mixtec migrants to sponsor development projects back in their home village of Soyaltepec. Not only did Mixtec out-migrants provide monetary and moral support toward this end but also some Mixtecs in Mexico City eventually ran for municipal office back home and, when elected, actually returned to Oaxaca to serve their terms. Thus, Orellana's explanation has cultural, political, and economic dimensions that span the points of origin and destination.

Yet another example of a resource-competition perspective comes from the publications of Dutch sociologist Fred Jongkind, who gathered data mainly among rural migrants in the urban setting of Lima, Peru. In a 1974 publication, Jongkind attacked the pioneering work of Mangin and Doughty. Arguing, first, that "regional clubs" (as he put it) vary greatly in the size of the territorial division on which they are based, Jongkind denied that more than 10 percent of the total Lima population associated in a tangible form with their fellow migrants. Jongkind also denied that regional clubs made any substantive, sustained contribution to the development of home villages or regions. Instead, Jongkind proposed that "the regional club is essentially elitist, composed of well-adjusted and successful migrants." Thus, the motive of migrant organizers, according to Jongkind, had more to do with their desire for social status and prestige in the urban setting than with facilitating their migrant compatriots or helping out the home village (Jongkind 1974:476).

Although this and subsequent articles (e.g., 1986) have had an impact on the field—especially in calling on researchers to reconsider the exclusively urban functions of regional associations—subsequent investigations have confirmed Mangin and Doughty's initial reports concerning the numbers and significance of migrant associations in Lima (e.g., Altamirano 1984a, 1984b; Golte and Adams 1987; also, see Doughty 1976 for Doughty's response to Jongkind).

From the perspective of resource competition, if migrants' position within the urban setting is initially low, associations provide a vehicle for them to share information and resources as a group. Insofar as their regional organization facilitates greater access to urban resources, it can play a crucial role in the adaptation of individuals and the migrant community as a whole. This same perspective encompasses the alternative hypothesis that the leadership of migrant associations is an elite subset that is essentially in pursuit of status and prestige. Either way, it should be noted that this perspective also has the strength of allowing us to place ethnographic descriptions of migrant regional associations into the context of urban economic and political systems. Migrant leaders and organizations can thus be understood as "actors" who are able to plan, organize, and in some cases actually shape their individual and collective destinies.

Structuralist Views

Structuralist perspectives posit that capitalist programs of industrialization, which in Latin America have typically confined growth to one or only a few urban centers, have produced a pattern of unequal development (Armstrong and McGee 1985). Since uneven development in the Third World is deleterious to the rural periphery, inequities between the city and the country are a central part of the dynamic that stimulates out-migration from the provinces. Differing levels of economic development and economic and political articulation with the region and the nation thus produce different contexts for out-migration and for rural–urban linkages on the part of migrants. Although structuralist frameworks are largely macro oriented and sometimes do not offer hypotheses pertinent to the ethnographic settings that anthropologists often study, one outstanding longitudinal study in Peru, carried out by Norman Long, Bryan Roberts, and their colleagues, provides a systematic set of hypotheses well worth considering here.

Roberts and Long propose that migrant associations fully reflect the relationship between the "city and the provinces," especially in terms of economic linkages between the two, and that migrant adaptations and organizations can best be studied and analyzed within this larger context. One of the classic applications of this approach is presented in a 1974 article by Roberts that compares patterns of urban adaptation on the part of rural migrants in Lima with those found in Guatemala City. In Peru, the indigenous peasant migrants Roberts studied came from communities with a strong tradition of cooperation and mutual aid. In the Peruvian communities of origin, there is a process of regional economic development and economic opportunity, and an open political structure that allows considerable regional autonomy. By contrast, Guatemalan *ladinos* (people of mixed Spanish and Indian descent) come from communities where there is a much greater degree of class stratification and economic stagnation. The political structure is also less independent of external authority, more rigid, and thus less accessible.

Patterns of migration and urban adaptation follow conditions in the points of origin. Peruvian Indians migrate in order to sustain people and enterprises back home; consequently, they maintain close ties with their villages of origin. As a result, Roberts sees migration (and the migrants themselves) as an "extension of economic and social fields of activity" that unite the city and the hinterlands. In contrast, when *ladinos* migrate to Guatemala City they often cut their ties and rarely return home, even for visits.

In terms of class dynamics, Roberts proposes that migration in Peru initially involved "middle" strata peasants who had land and who were thus interested in development in their communities of origin. Migrant associations often were set up either by resident traders in Peruvian cities or by urban professional elites. These associations, which date back to the early 1900s, helped organize temporary laborers in the city but were also involved in land disputes, disputes over political jurisdictions and regional political hierarchies, and the process of village and regional development back in the provinces.

During the 1970s, Roberts, Long, and a team of colleagues, expanded upon this research, focusing on the impact of capitalistic economic penetration and development on rural villages in the Mantaro Valley in Peru (Long and Roberts 1978, 1984). These and associated studies confirmed that special rural–urban ties proliferated between the capital city of Lima and the surrounding agricultural districts and villages due to the weak and dependent pattern of national development in Peru (Long 1973; Long and Roberts 1978, 1984; and Roberts 1981). Roberts states that, in this context, migrant village and regional associations "are but one part of the institutional matrix that accompanies Lima's industrialization. Kinship ties, ties based on place of origin or fictive kinship ties . . . are also emphasized. . . . These provide the contacts for obtaining cheap supplies and for mobilizing labor" (Roberts 1981: 38). Roberts argues that conditions favoring the formation of migrant associations are intensified because of the "pendular" nature of migration from the highlands, with migrants frequently traveling back and forth between the city and the provinces. The range and frequency of rural–urban ties are also effectively accounted for, in that "associational activities, religious celebrations and kinship gatherings provide a cultural context in which relationships needed for economic survival can be consolidated" (Roberts 1981:38).[12]

Teófilo Altamirano, a former fieldworker for and doctoral student of Long and Roberts during the 1970s, expanded further upon this same approach in his comprehensive study of Peruvian migrant associations in Lima (1984a). Altamirano particularly examined the evolution of associations from the Mantaro Valley, noting that they were increasingly characterized by class divisions. On the one hand, there were migrant associations dominated by middle-class migrants who were more interested in urban and class-oriented issues than issues concerning their communities of origin. Migrants from the smaller communities in the Mantaro Valley, however, continued to be involved in political struggles based in the point of origin, which, in fact, often had to do with winning increased political and economic autonomy from the larger regional centers.

In summary, structuralist perspectives emphasize the inequality manifest in regional disparities between the city and the provinces as the dynamic that generates out-migration and that can influence migrant social organization as well. Eventually, however, class differences inherent in the organization of the provinces may themselves generate conflict and division as distinct political positions evolve. As Altamirano puts it, migrant associations are "diverse in their origins, organization and functions, since contemporary processes of migration include regions of very different levels of socio-economic development and, within regions, people who exhibit different economic and political interests" (1984b:216).

CONCLUSION

As a formalized manifestation of regional ties and commitments among migrants from the same place, it is worth noting that the perspectives and hypotheses on migrant associations delineated above are not mutually exclusive. Rather, they are best thought of as alternative ways of looking at the same behavior.

The sociopsychological perspective involves at least four hypotheses about the formation and functions of migrant regional associations:

1. Migrant associations play an important role in acclimating the new migrant to life in the city and thus help to bridge the gap between the social, cultural, and political life of their points of origin and destination.
2. Migrant associations provide a comfortable and relatively secure linguistic, cultural, and social environment for new migrants.
3. Migrant associations provide a social field for migrants to extend provincial culture and practices to the urban setting.
4. Migrant associations sometimes allow self-regulation of the membership and reinforce culturally specific norms and values.

Note that the sociopsychological perspective encompasses two potentially contradictory views. On the one hand, given the above hypotheses, it could be argued that migrant associations help their members make a positive transition to life in the city; that is, that migrant associations are socially integrative. On the other hand, it could also be argued that migrant associations ultimately retard integration by encapsulating migrants into networks made up primarily of compatriots and thus isolating them from interaction with members of the larger society (see, e.g., Romer 1982:114).

The resource-competition perspective generates the following hypotheses about the formation and functions of migrant associations:

1. Migrant associations are most likely to form in situations in which migrants lack access to basic urban resources such as employment, housing, a modicum of self-determination, social and recreational activities, and status.
2. Associations cohere primarily because the migrant group is advancing or defending special interests, whether economic or political.

Scholars differ over the status and class situation of the migrants who are most likely to form and participate in migrant associations. Some argue that regional associations are formed by migrants who find themselves at the very bottom of the urban economic and political structure. Others believe that an elite stratum within the migrant community utilizes migrant associations as a way of enhancing their prestige and personal power (which, again, they might not have access to within the larger urban system). Concomitantly, these scholars believe, the less fortunate have neither the time nor the resources to participate fully. Jongkind in particular has proposed that, because of this, migrant associations in Lima are neither effective nor truly meaningful in actually involving or helping the larger migrant population, or representing their real needs and interests.

Structuralist perspectives, remember, are based on the assumption that regional associations are primarily an organizational response to dependency stemming from unequal patterns of national and local development. Three central hypotheses follow from this assumption:

1. The economic and political structure of communities and regions of origin have a profound impact on the formation, form, and focus of migrant associations.
2. Often migrant associations are formed by migrants from the larger and more developed communities of a given region, who are also among the earliest to out-migrate.
3. Over time, class divisions become salient in migrant associations: those migrants from the wealthier regions or communities become more oriented toward the city and toward urban issues, while their less advantaged compatriots have a stronger commitment to regionalism and regional development per se back home.

Regarding the last hypothesis, Altamirano proposes that although class interests can be expected eventually to divide the original migrant association or federation, class interests also offer new possibilities for alliance with other groups in both the point of origin and in the city (see Altamirano 1984b).

Although structuralists have agreed about the origins of migrant associations and their dynamics, some difference of opinion has emerged among them as to the associations' political potential. Some scholars view migrant associations as politically progressive insofar as they deal with regional inequities. Given that dependent and uneven development are major problems throughout Latin America, migrant associations can provide the basis for a rhetoric for exposing inequities as well as a field for struggle and social change in order to address them (e.g., Altamirano 1984a; Slater 1989). Other scholars have implied that migrant associations are retrograde to the extent that regional hierarchies are replicated in the city, as migrants from the regional economic and political centers try to organize and dominate migrants from the hinterlands (e.g., Arizpe 1978:27).

In summary, it is clear that migrant associations can serve a range of important moral and material functions.[13] It is also possible that, under certain conditions, they offer bases for exploitation if fundamentally egalitarian principles are manipulated and subverted by those with explicit or hidden class or political agendas.

To further clarify the above issues, as well as to address the broader question of when a given group of rural–urban migrants is likely to form a migrant association based on principles of paisanazgo, it is helpful to turn now to a detailed set of case studies of mutual aid and associations among Mountain Zapotec migrants. This will, in turn, allow us to address more effectively the broader issue of the uses of paisanazgo among urban migrants from indigenous peasant backgrounds in Latin America.

PART II

Mountain Zapotec Life in the Region and the Capital

CHAPTER 3

The Rural–Urban Interface

This chapter presents a historical overview of the Mountain Zapotec, specifically the way the course of national development has affected the Sierra Juárez region where they live. It also outlines salient features of the economic development of Mexico City, since it has been the primary point of urban destination for Mountain Zapotec out-migrants from the 1950s through the 1980s. Finally, it offers an account of why and how I collected the material on which this book is based and describes the strengths and weaknesses of the data I have used.

HISTORICAL OVERVIEW OF THE MOUNTAIN ZAPOTEC

The Mountain Zapotec live in the northern part of the State of Oaxaca, primarily in the district of Villa Alta, an officially constituted administrative unit that currently includes some twenty-five municipalities. Although quite removed from the state capital of Oaxaca City, largely because of the rugged Sierra Madre mountains, it is clear that the Zapotec villages of the sierra were for a long time an integral part of the Spanish colonial economy.

Soon after they overran the Triple Alliance in 1521, the Spanish conquistadores began to explore the sierra, and over the next thirty years in the lands over which they gained control, they enforced policies of resettlement, religious conversion, political reorganization, and economic extraction (Chance 1989:16–20). In addition to farming, indigenous populations were forced to provide labor, mine precious metals, and meet heavy production quotas of woven cloth. Tributes and forced sales via the institution of the *repartimiento* were so extensive that Spanish nobles and bureaucrats actively competed with each other to win the lucrative task of administering the district (Hamnett 1971).

It is worth noting that the postconquest roots of village-level identity stem in part from the forms of local political organization imposed by the Spaniards on the indigenous communities of the sierra. Under a royal policy known as La República de los Indios, the Spanish colonizers separated Indians into distinct communities, each of which was able to exercise a degree of self-governance based on local traditions and customs. This policy was part and parcel of a colonial system designed to divide and rule the indigenous population as well as to keep anyone from interfering with the Spanish Crown's royal prerogatives and interests (Nader 1989). In the twentieth century, such divisions and rights were codified into state law (Wolf 1967:306). It is relevant to note here that the state of Oaxaca, one of the most indigenous states in Mexico, is also one of the most administratively complex. An official census of 1986 notes that Oaxaca was divided into no less than 570 municipalities, or almost 24 percent of the nation's total.

According to Berg's account (1974), coffee was brought into the area in the late 1800s and because of its potential for generating cash income, its cultivation diffused up into the hinterlands. An increase in cash cropping resulted in a gradual shift from the local market, with its dependence on merchant capital, to commercial capital, which accompanied the adoption of new means of marketing agricultural crops and the establishment of individually owned stores in the larger towns (Young 1978a, 1982).

Following local disruptions during the Mexican Revolution, the period from the 1930s through the 1970s was characterized by increasingly strong ties to Oaxaca City, the state, and the larger Mexican nation. These ties initially took the form of an expansion of schools, post offices, and limited telephone service into the region during the 1930s. Some of the sierra communities were affected by the *bracero* program, which by a special agreement between Mexico and the United States during World War II allowed Mexicans a temporary permit to live and work in the United States and supplement the labor force there (see Berg 1974:226–27 and Weaver and Downing 1976). The most significant development, however, occurred with the construction of roads into the sierra during the 1950s, which allowed greater export of cash crops and the importation of new consumer goods into the area. Infrastructure and services were further extended throughout the 1960s in the form of increasingly effective health care services, electricity, potable-water systems, and the placement in the sierra's larger towns of government offices, like INMECAFE, the Mexican government's coffee institute, which both advised farmers and purchased their crop. Today the Zapotec population of the sierra lives in dispersed communities. The majority of settlements are small, and most communities prefer endogamous marriage (i.e., marriage to fellow villagers). In 1970, out of fifty-six locales included in the census of the district of Villa Alta, 55 percent (or thirty-one communities) had populations between 1 and 500. Only one town had more than 2,000 persons. Some communities in the district are quite compact, while others are spread out (Nader 1964).

Politically and administratively, the communities of the sierra are organized into semiautonomous legal and political municipalities. Each municipal unit is composed of a main town or village and a number of dependencies, including smaller villages, hamlets, *haciendas,* and *ranchos.* The population of a municipal unit has the power to elect a self-administering government. Municipal units are arranged into larger districts for administrative purposes by the state of Oaxaca (Greenberg 1990).

Because there is variation among the individual communities in this area, I eschew further generalizations about them. Rather, descriptions of three specific communities in the following chapter—Lahoya, an agricultural village; Ralu'a, the primary local marketing center of the Rincón; and Villa Alta, the district seat—will provide insight into the range of the region's settlement types, populations, economies, and forms of political and social organization, as well as levels of development. In order to comprehend the impact of the Mexican State upon development in the Sierra Juárez in more detail, it is necessary first to review official government interpretations of, and responses to, the indigenous question in general.

THE MEXICAN STATE AND THE INCORPORATION OF INDIGENOUS COMMUNITIES

Throughout the twentieth century Mexican history has been characterized by an ideology of nationalism and a program of national development (Wolf 1959). The components were created after the 1910 Revolution and continued, albeit waxing and waning in intensity, into the 1980s. Principal among these were land reform, the effort to modernize agricultural production, and government programs to encourage the development of the national infrastructure. In addition, the Mexican government promoted popular education and literacy; the extension of broader political rights, such as voting, to the masses; and the incorporation of Mexican Indians into the national mainstream.

Concern over the sociocultural integration of Indians had its roots in the 1910 Revolution. The postrevolutionary formation of a national ideology based on the new power of the mestizos heralded an era in which the indigenous past of Mexico was not just accepted but lauded. Intellectuals such as the anthropologist Manuel Gamio were influential in this regard. As early as

1915, Gamio called for study of the Indian condition as the basis for "social integration." Subsequently, the federal government established a number of rural schools and cultural missions in the 1920s and 1930s. The harsh realities facing indigenous peoples made revisionist ideologies and programs problematic, and, not surprisingly, these institutions generally failed at their assigned tasks.

According to Ralph L. Beals, Mexico's Indigenista movement had at least three lines of development: the romanticist, based on the view that Indian culture could be restored to its pristine state; the rehabilitationist, which focused on the economic and political realms; and finally the assimilationist, which sought to incorporate Mexico's Indian peoples into the national mainstream through direct educational and other interventionist work. Up to the 1940s, work along all three lines proved frustrating. Indians certainly did not respond cooperatively or fully to programs of "national uniformity in culture." Beals faults unimaginative officials, who "perceived the problem essentially to be one of introducing symbols of 'modernism,' progress and Mexicanness" (1967:465; see also Knight 1990).

The rehabilitationist and assimilationist methods that became dominant during the regime of Mexican president Lázaro Cárdenas between 1934 and 1940, treated Indian communities as corporate entities to be dealt with through special programs and offices. These efforts were based on the assumption that, in the long run, this was a more efficacious way of making Indians part of the nation, in contrast to the simple Liberal preference for "elimination though economic destruction" (Adams 1967:477).

Somewhat more sensitive, and perhaps more effective, were post–World War II efforts along the same lines by the Instituto Nacional Indigenista (INI), and by projects initiated under the auspices of international agencies such as UNESCO and the OAS. Regarding the former, Beals wrote: "The Instituto Nacional Indigenista program concentrates on improved and more realistic educational facilities, health programs, agriculture, and communications, but makes no direct effort to manipulate the social structure or symbolic and belief systems" (Beals 1967:466).[1] Other critics have offered less charitable interpretations of such efforts. Dunbar Ortiz, for example, argues that official Indian advocacy in Mexico has been characterized by an emphasis on fundamentally integrationist policies. Furthermore, "[i]ntegration ideology does not distinguish among ethnic groups, but rather sees them within a unitary national framework as 'peasants' (*campesinos*) or 'natives', assuming that there must be an 'upward' racial and cultural mixing of Indians with the rest of the population in order to overcome their 'backwardness', that is, their Indianness" (Dunbar Ortiz 1984:79). Similarly, Adams notes that in Mexico, "[t]he Indianists, then as now, aim toward elimination of the Indian as a socially corporate entity within the body politic" (Adams 1967:477).

It is interesting that these ideological debates, and the policies and agencies that resulted from them, have had only a minimal impact on peripheral rural areas like the Villa Alta district. Thus the connection between the nation and the Sierra Juárez must be reconstructed from available historical materials.

DEVELOPMENT IN THE VILLA ALTA DISTRICT OF THE SIERRA JUÁREZ

One of the outstanding items on the agenda of the Mexican Revolution had to do with land reform and the creation of new holdings for the peasantry. Land reform measures, however, had no impact on this part of the Sierra Juárez of Oaxaca. While nominally owned by each community, most land was held in small, individually operated parcels rather than large haciendas or plantations.

The construction of basic infrastructure in the region was slow and gradual from the 1930s through the 1950s. As lines of communication and transportation improved, the production of coffee and other cash crops such as sugar, pepper, and avocados steadily increased. Nonetheless, the Mountain Zapotec's direct contact with the Mexican government, whether state or federal, was minimal. Nader reports that taxes were only sporadically collected before the mid-1950s, and administrative and educational matters in the region were essentially left to Villa Alta, the state's officially designated district seat.[2]

Since the end of World War II, a major impetus for regional development in the portion of the Sierra Juárez where the Mountain Zapotec reside has come in the form of the Papaloapan Commission. This commission was set up in 1947 under the administration of Mexican president Miguel Alemán (1946–1952) and got rolling in the early 1950s. As a federal agency, it was given a broad set of powers, including the right to "plan . . . and construct all works for flood control, irrigation, power generation, communication—including water transport, ports, roads, railroads, telegraphs, and telephones—and urbanization in the area" (Poleman 1964:95). According to Poleman, change and progress were quite slow in the beginning, largely because of the general backwardness of the agricultural sector in the Papaloapan basin.

The commission took a new direction in 1952 under the revitalized administration of the next Mexican president, Ruiz Cortines (1952–1958). Under his leadership, efforts were redirected away from previous priorities—such as flood control, drainage, and irrigation—and redoubled in areas like roads and airfields, linking the hinterlands to the state government, agricultural development, and "the Commission's education and sanitary engineering operations" (Poleman 1964:107). Achievements in the former category include direct aid to almost four hundred rural primary schools. In terms of sanitation, water purification efforts helped curtail major illnesses resulting from either malaria or intestinal parasites.[3]

More recent research indicates that the commission's work actually devastated indigenous populations in the core areas of the project (Partridge et al. 1982; Boege 1988), but on the periphery of the commission's domain—specifically in Villa Alta—the results were much more salubrious. In 1964, Nader commented:

> In the 1950's . . . under the auspices of the Papaloapan Commission, road engineers, agronomists, medical specialists, and educators were sent to all of the Rincon villages as part of an all-out integrated program to develop the Oaxacan zone. . . . In addition to practical accomplishments, such as finally connecting the Rincon by road to the valley of Oaxaca, initiating coffee nurseries, and improving and sanitizing the water supply to various villages, the Papaloapan Commission was an important catalytic agent. (Nader 1964:214)

In summary, it is worth noting that, outside of those Zapotecs who went north as part of the bracero program during World War II and those who felt the effects of the Papaloapan Commission, direct contact with federal or state agencies or officials has generally been limited, with the notable exception of some towns like Ralu'a. Contact with and knowledge of Mexican culture filtered in chiefly through Zapotec merchants with commercial ties or interests outside of the sierra, or through elementary-school teachers or official intermediaries—often bilingual and bicultural Zapotecs from the district seat or adjacent districts (Nader 1964:214). Thus, the effects of the Mexican government's integrationist policies, at least in the diluted forms in which they reached the sierra before the 1950s, were apparently confined largely to education.[4]

The historical-structural matrix of "modernization" and "integration" in the Sierra Juárez was thus a somewhat belated rural corollary of an intensive program of national development that focused on the industrialization of Mexico City (Unikel et al. 1976). In this sense, national efforts toward industrialization—which during the 1950s was centered in the capital and aimed at implementing a policy of import substitution—as well as the effort to integrate the rural periphery with the rest of the nation, were dual expressions of the increasing centralization of the Mexican state. This same process created a tremendous demand for labor in Mexico City at the same time that rural occupational opportunities in the Oaxacan highlands, especially in proportion to the population base, were quite limited in all but the main rural administrative or commercial centers.

Concomitantly, case studies of the Oaxacan highlands indicate four features that distinguish the communities of this region from others in Mexico, such as those found in the central highlands: (1) a notable tendency toward municipal autonomy and self-governance; (2) a means of production characterized by small-scale, nonmechanized, labor-intensive agriculture; and

(3) an increasing but still essentially peripheral connection to a capitalist mode of production. Insofar as the last feature is concerned, the greatest influence has occurred in the growing importance of cash cropping and commerce (Young 1978a).

High rates of out-migration have characterized the sierra as a whole. One estimate indicates that so many people left between 1960 and 1970 that the annual growth rate was reduced to 1.18 percent (Cabrera Acevedo 1975). This tendency certainly characterized the three sierran communities examined here, although research indicates that the population of the district of Villa Alta (with an annual growth rate of 3.2 percent) apparently increased enough during the same period for it to be labeled a rural area that was "attracting" in-migrants (Nolasco 1979, 1:150).

MEXICO CITY AS URBAN CONTEXT

Since Mexico City was the predominant urban destination of out-migrants from the Sierra Juárez from the mid-1950s to the mid-1980s, it is appropriate to outline some of the Federal District's most salient features at this point, especially because the literature indicates that these have had an impact on rural–urban migrants.[5]

The first phase of Mountain Zapotec migration to Mexico City was of limited size, lasted until about 1958, and coincided with the development of a dynamic urban industrial economy. The growth of the economy in the first phase of industrial development was linked to the production of nondurable consumer goods (Muñoz, Oliveira, and Stern 1977:30). Along with the growth of the primary and secondary sectors of the economy, the capital was also the center of many tertiary services and activities, all supplementing industrial growth and production.

The main sources of migrants during this period were either nearby cities, which were not developing, or areas of subsistence agriculture in the central highlands surrounding the capital. Migrants from the nearby cities were usually skilled workers who came to Mexico City in search of better wages in nonmanual occupations. Migrants from the areas of subsistence agriculture, on the other hand, went into unskilled occupations in industry and the tertiary sector (Muñoz, Oliveira, and Stern 1977:52).

From 1950 to 1960, along with a shift toward the mass consumption of capital goods, there was a gradual reduction of both industrial growth in and migration to the capital. Muñoz, Oliveira, and Stern interpret this trend as a significant change in the strategy and pattern of economic development.

Subsequent patterns of development from 1960 to 1970 reversed this trend, with increases in both industrial growth and migration (Muñoz, Oliveira, and Stern 1977:51). The composition of the migrants to the capital also changed.

By the 1960s, migration streams came increasingly from the rural and relatively deprived regions of Mexico (Muñoz, Oliveira, and Stern 1977:43). In fact, the size and state of development in the points of origin, as well as the educational levels of the migrants, declined during this decade. In addition, since the 1960s, migration streams to the capital have been over increasing distances.

Heavy industry, the most dynamic sector of industrial manufacturing in the capital, also absorbed the largest proportion of rural migrants between 1950 and 1970 (Oliveira 1976). Research indicates that industrial growth was so extensive that even men with low educational levels and older men were able to find unskilled jobs in this sector even if they had no previous industrial work experience. The different branches of the service sector directly related to industrial production also expanded during this period, and they absorbed more of the labor force than the rest of the tertiary sector combined. Thus the entrance of rural migrants into the occupational sector of the capital during the 1960s and 1970s was concentrated in unskilled jobs in the manufacturing sector of the urban economy. As such, migrants played a key role in the formation of an industrial proletariat. At the same time, it is significant that migrants were *not* being forced into marginalized service occupations in the tertiary sector of the urban economy (Muñoz, Oliveira, and Stern 1977:50–55).

During the 1970s, however, the occupational structure of the capital became increasingly "crystallized," making entry into nonmanual industrial occupations unlikely for recently arrived migrants. Crystallization also resulted in "credentialism," in which the amount and quality of one's schooling became key mechanisms in determining social stratification (Stern 1982).

By 1950, then, Mexico City had evolved into the most industrialized city in the nation, reaffirming its role as the undisputed center of economic, political, and cultural life.[6] As conditions deteriorated in the countryside, especially on the periphery, where subsistence and self-provisioning styles of agriculture were practiced, millions of peasants were in effect "pushed" out of agricultural villages and "pulled" to the capital, where the industrialization process demanded large amounts of skilled and unskilled labor. Because dependent capitalism created a pattern of unequal national development, the capital could offer substantially better opportunities, wages, and lifestyles than any other urban point of destination within Mexico, especially for unskilled laborers (Schteingart 1988). This resulted in a highly favorable situation for incoming migrants that—along with the general stages of economic growth described above—must certainly be taken into account when evaluating the experience and patterns of Mountain Zapotec urban adaptation.

During the 1960s and 1970s, the macro-structural context of rural–urban migration to Mexico City was framed by a combination of forces, including growing population pressures, the continuing deterioration of the economic situation (especially agriculture) in rural areas, and the continuing need for skilled and unskilled labor in Mexico City. In light of these factors, a majority of the new migrants to the capital between 1960 and 1980 were probably from rural, agricultural, and often indigenous backgrounds. In this sense, the Mountain Zapotec were part and parcel of the large rural exodus from remote parts of the nation that had not previously been important sources of out-migration.

FIELDWORK: GATHERING THE DATA

Sociocultural anthropologists often gather data through the firsthand observation and study of a culture over an extended period. Based as it is on a combination of interviewing and participant observation, this process, called fieldwork, has been and continues to be the main strategy for data collection in sociocultural anthropological research.[7]

Ethnography is both the purpose and the product of fieldwork. Essentially a descriptive task, ethnography results in the framing of a given topic within a holistic perspective that the anthropologist obtains by studying the larger culture and society. Ideally, through the same process the skilled anthropologist can generate analytical and theoretical concepts that are useful beyond the particular case being studied.

An ethnographic approach to the study of migration and urban adaptation is the main research method I used to collect the information presented in Part 2.[8] For this reason, an account of how I collected data best illustrates the nature of this approach, as well as the relative strengths and weaknesses of my data.[9] The data on which this book is based were originally gathered for a doctoral dissertation in anthropology at the University of California at Berkeley, but the present study differs in important respects from the dissertation, so an indication of the focus and scope of the latter is relevant here as well.

In 1974, during my first year of graduate studies, Professor Laura Nader informed me that out-migration from the Mountain Zapotec area of the Sierra Juárez Mountains to other parts of Mexico and to the United States was steadily increasing. At that time, none of the available studies on the Zapotec focused specifically on this phenomenon, nor had any detailed studies been published focusing on how Zapotec migrants were adapting to life in the city. Thus, one of the principal reasons I became interested in this topic was to document and analyze the scope, causes, and effects of Mountain Zapotec migration. Another reason was that Professor Nader had studied a number of villages in the area, and her research could provide a foundation and a baseline for the study of social change. Third, and a matter of no small importance, this choice allowed me to build upon the many contacts and the rapport that Professor Nader had already established with the Mountain Zapotec. Because of her work and reputation, I was in a position to gather more and better-quality data in a shorter time and with less difficulty than if I had initiated my research independently.

On this basis, I carried out two summers of exploratory fieldwork. I spent the summer of 1975 in the Mountain Zapotec village of Ralu'a, studying outmigration.[10] Since my research indicated that most of the Ralu'ans who had left were in Mexico City, I spent the summer of 1976 in the capital, locating and interviewing as many Ralu'ans as I could find.

After completing these exploratory projects, I returned to Mexico City in July 1977 to begin the fieldwork for my doctoral dissertation. The theoretical orientation of the proposed research involved a critique of the modernization approach to social change and development. The modernization approach—which in one form posits that assimilation to Western, industrial, and universal values is central to the modernization process—neglected the positive aspects of group-oriented strategies of cooperation and mobility. As Janice E. Perlman has pointed out, "While modernization theorists differ on details, they agree that strong family ties, extended kinship networks, or 'loyalties to family and clan' serve to hinder individual mobility, constrain individual achievement, limit an individual's economic advancement, and take precedence over the individual's loyalty to his nation" (1976:113).

Contrary to the modernizationists' position, my fieldwork suggested that the migrants from Ralu'a provided an example of group-oriented adaptation that had resulted in rapid socioeconomic and educational mobility. In conducting the research for this study, I intended to focus on three topics: (1) patterns of migration, (2) patterns and broad changes in urban social organization, and (3) group-oriented strategies for mobility. Specifically, I intended to test the hypothesis that aspects of the rural background of the Ralu'an migrants—including rural communal strategies of cooperation such as *tequio* (unpaid labor that each male citizen provides to support civic projects) and *gozona* (the exchange of labor between individuals)—were critical variables in understanding this group's communal orientation toward the challenges of daily life in Mexico City.

To gather data systematically, I used a questionnaire written by Professor Perlman as a basis for an intensive survey investigation.[11] This questionnaire had the advantage that it was comprehensive enough for use as a general social survey (it included, for example, sections on worldview, politics, economics, migration and adaptation, housing and household possessions, and background biographical data) while also allowing for the diachronic study of migration and of the occupational histories of informants. Once I had drafted and tested several translations of this questionnaire, I drew a list of sample names from a census of all the known heads of households from Ralu'a in Mexico City. I got in touch with a university student who had helped me make contacts the summer before. Our agreement was that he would help me find migrants during weekends, and I would set up interviews for the following week.

After making contact with a potential informant, I explained my purpose; provided a page of information outlining the content of the questionnaire, its confidentiality, my academic affiliation in Mexico, and my address; and then asked for an interview and a date when it would be possible to return and administer the questionnaire.[12] I also continued to supplement my formal interviews by conducting informal conversations with both individuals and groups and by participating in events of migrant community life: visiting, dinners, parties, basketball and soccer games where the teams were made up of youth from the town, dances, weddings, and the like. I continued to develop and consult with a group of key informants, some of whom were willing to give me extended life histories. As my survey data accumulated, I found it useful to ask for detailed commentary and interpretation on certain themes from these key informants. I also consulted them to get information on topics that I considered too sensitive to ask about in a formal interview situation—for example, the formation of cliques and intragroup or intrafamily grievances and conflict resolution.

When I initiated fieldwork in 1977, I estimated that there were about 150 households in Mexico City made up primarily of Ralu'an migrants, for a total of from four to five hundred adults over the age of eighteen. By 1978 I had met representatives from eighty of these households, and among them I was able to conduct sixty-five personal interviews about the process of migration and urban adaptation, most of which were based on the extensive questionnaire. These sixty-five interviews with members of sixty different households, were taken in a nonrandom sample that represented a little more than one-third of the known Ralu'an households. Although obtaining a true random sample was not possible, I made an effort to interview a wide variety of informants. The variables considered in this regard included age, type of neighborhood, occupation, and socioeconomic level. I did my best to interview as many women as I could, but my access to both married and single women was somewhat limited because of my gender and marital status. These interviews, which were again supplemented with informal methods, provided the data on migration, adaptation, and the contemporary Ralu'an community in Mexico City.[13]

By 1978, after a year of solid fieldwork, many of my initial impressions about the Ralu'an migrants were confirmed. According to most of the Mountain Zapotecs I talked to, the Ralu'an migrants formed a large, cohesive community in Mexico City. The Ralu'an migrants themselves maintained that the key characteristic of their group was the amount of mutual aid exchanged among migrants and directed toward the village. The central characteristic of the Ralu'an migrants as a whole was their relative economic and occupational achievement in the capital, a fact that I was able to confirm through an analysis of salary levels and the rate of union membership. On the basis of this information, the hypothesized relationship between adaptation in Mexico City and patterns and networks of mutual aid between migrants appeared to be substantiated.

To gain a better sense of how broadly representative the Ralu'an case was, I spent the first part of the following year doing survey work on migrants in Mexico City from a number of villages in the immediate vicinity of Ralu'a. Two things became apparent: first, the number of migrants from all but a few neighboring villages was much smaller than the number from Ralu'a, and second, the migrants from these other villages—with a few exceptions—seemed to adjust more slowly to Mexico City and on the whole seemed to do less well in terms of occupational and educational attainment.

The main case in point was a group of migrants from a village I will call Lahoya. Preliminary interviews indicated that the male migrants from Lahoya frequently worked as laborers in the "informal" sector of the urban economy or as workers in relatively unskilled occupations in the formal sector.[14] These men also reported short- to long-term periods of unemployment. In contrast, many single women from Lahoya came to work in Mexico City as maids and appeared to do relatively well. Along with these differences, I also learned that the migrants from Lahoya tended to cluster in a few neighborhoods on the periphery of the city, especially in the eastern and southern quadrants. Finally, the Lahoyans in Mexico City had formed a number of strong migrant associations devoted to the development of the village back home.

Further research revealed that the population in Mexico City from the village of Lahoya in 1978 was about three hundred adult migrants. Two circumstances impeded my making an accurate estimate of the total population and selecting a large sample from this group. First, since there has traditionally been either friction or mutual disregard between the two communities, the fact that I had worked with the Ralu'an migrants made some of the Lahoyans suspicious of my motives. Second, at the time I started fieldwork, the Lahoyan migrant community in Mexico City and Lahoyans back in the village were divided into antagonistic factions, thus producing a tense climate.

As a result of this situation, data collection among the Lahoyan migrants took the following form. Initially I made contact with the leaders of all the factions and conducted long, open-ended interviews on the reasons for migration and the present situation of their fellow villagers in the capital. Then I selected a small number of key informants whom I interviewed in great depth over a period of six months. I verified and expanded on the information gathered in this manner by interviewing thirty-five nonrandomly selected migrants from three key neighborhoods where there was a pattern of residential clustering. I supplemented information gathered in this fashion with data from the national census and government archives.

These comments should give some idea of the limitations of the Lahoyan data. The Lahoyan migrant sample was small and nonrandom, access was sometimes limited, and it was difficult to cross-check or verify data with conventional methods. I also gathered the bulk of the Lahoyan data over the period of a year, compared to the eighteen months spread over five years that I spent among the Ralu'ans. On the whole, I believe I talked to Lahoyan migrants who were more attached to both to their compatriots in Mexico City and their home village. I basically had no access to Lahoyan women and only managed to interview a few on the side at larger gatherings.

Finally, two additional caveats about how I gathered the data in both cases deserve mention here. First, while most Zapotec migrants associate with *capitalinos* from many different spheres in the urban system, their kin and paisanos were clearly their central point of reference. At an analytical level, this fact allowed me to study Mountain Zapotec migrant groups from the various villages and towns as if they were relatively distinct, self-contained communities even though from either a spatial or a behavioral point of view this was not actually the case. This device was of crucial importance in a city that was then inhabited by more than twelve million people. Unlike a rural community, where many aspects of public life can be observed firsthand, some arbitrary boundaries must be imposed if an anthropologist is to carry out a study in a major metropolitan area.

In addition, my focus here is on groups and networks rather than individuals despite the fact that I was fortunate to meet a good number of extraordinary persons among the Mountain Zapotecs in Mexico City and that I am aware that a complete ethnography of the social and political organization of these migrants would require additional description and analysis of community leaders. Ethical considerations resulting from a concern to respect the principle of informed consent as well as confidentiality dictate a more sociological style of presentation than I might otherwise have preferred.

In terms of the data base for the third case study, although I never had the opportunity to visit Villa Alta, I did ask both Ralu'ans and Lahoyans about Villaltecos in Mexico City and managed to talk to a few out-migrants from there. Fortunately, in 1988 anthropologist Philip C. Parnell, who went through the doctoral program in anthropology at the University of California at Berkeley a few years ahead of me, published a fascinating study of the town of Villa Alta. Much of the data concerning Villalteco out-migrants reported in Parnell's book were collected in a 1984 re-visit after he graduated, supplementing information presented in his 1978 doctoral dissertation. At any rate, the new information Parnell presented enabled me to take a more comparative regional perspective than I had been able to attain previously. The data on both Villa Alta and its out-migrants, then, are primarily from Parnell's book, supplemented by other published and unpublished materials in my possession.

The above account should enable the reader to understand and evaluate the ways in which I collected the data for this book and thus the ways in which biases may have impacted my descriptions and analyses. Certainly the intense and extended periods of contact that I had with the Zapotec make it difficult for me to be satisfied with *any* single interpretation of their lives or communities. This book, then, highlights but one of the many possible vantage points on the richness and strengths, as well as the possible weaknesses, that characterize the manifestations of contemporary Zapotec culture described here.

CHAPTER 4

The Communities of Origin

The previous chapter placed the Sierra Juárez in the context of the Mexican government's efforts to incorporate indigenous populations and communities into the national mainstream, particularly with respect to the economic development programs from the 1950s through the 1980s as they affected the Villa Alta district, where the Mountain Zapotec communities described below are located. Here, particular attention is given to three specific communities in the Villa Alta district that exhibit a range of levels of sociocultural integration with the state and the nation.

LAHOYA: AN AGRICULTURAL VILLAGE

Lahoya was a preconquest Zapotec settlement. It is likely that the village was moved by the Spaniards and that, over time, a number of neighboring villages were merged with it in a pacification process known as *congregación*. The limited data available suggest that during the nineteenth century Lahoya was a somewhat poor, subsistence-oriented agricultural village with a fluctuating but gradually increasing population.[1] According to national and community-level census data for the period since World War II, the population of the village reached a peak of 934 persons in 1950 (Dirección General de Estadística [hereafter DGE] 1954) and then dropped to 836 in 1960 and 676 in 1970. It was reportedly down to 416 persons in 1980, of which only 150 men could be counted as *ciudadanos*, or citizens. Interviews and data gathered in the community itself suggest that the population decline over the past thirty years was due largely to high rates of out-migration (see Instituto Nacional de Estadística Geografía e Informática [hereafter INEGI] 1984).

In the first three decades of the century, conditions were extremely difficult in Lahoya. There were boundary conflicts with neighboring villages and terrible periods of disease and epidemic. Poverty and hunger were common. Life was especially hard for those whose lands were poor or otherwise of limited value. This general situation led some families to leave Lahoya around 1936 in hope of establishing a better life in one of the other villages of the district. According to the migrants I spoke with in Mexico City, conditions changed between the early 1930s and the mid-1950s, when sugarcane (which could be processed into *panela,* or unrefined brown sugar) became a major cash crop in Lahoya.

The production of panela is reputedly the most strenuous process in local agricultural production. After the sugarcane is grown and harvested—the latter task requiring a work group of at least four people—the cane must be pressed. A special pressing machine (a *trapiche*) is used for this job, and if they are not owned, oxen must be rented to run it. Much firewood is also gathered, since the sugar juice has to boil continuously for hours. Once most of the liquid has evaporated, the residue is poured into molds and is left to harden. For a period of a few weeks the family-based teams work constantly, with very little sleep, in order to complete the process satisfactorily.

Despite such trials, making panela was very profitable because, before the mid-1950s, the product was in great demand. Traders from such diverse sierran villages as Tanetze, Juquila, Lachatao, and San Miguel del Río sought Lahoyan panela. They would sometimes arrive with as many as fifteen burros, carrying in all sorts of goods to trade. Then they would take the panela to the sierra mining town of Natividad and sell it at a profit.

Unfortunately, the panela boom did not last. National legislation promoted by the Mexican government during the 1940s worked to the disadvantage of the small, independent sugar farmers (Corbett and Whiteford 1983:22–28). The extensive fertile fields of the Valley of Oaxaca were more easily modernized and were closer to the routes of trade and transportation. Competition from farms in the valley undercut Lahoya's market for panela, and by the late 1950s the village had entered a period of economic stagnation intensified by high rates of out-migration, a good proportion of which involved the young men and women of the community. Despite modest development efforts, the village has never fully recovered from the collapse of its single economic boom. The village economy is now primarily based on a self-provisioning style of agriculture.[2] What is more, further development in Lahoya has also been curtailed because of its peripheral location (at least in terms of the entry of new roads and the resultant patterns of extraction and commerce) and its proximity to Ralu'a, the regional marketing center. Both circumstances have intensified the dependency of Lahoya on the latter.

Economic Base

Turning to the present economic base of the village, almost everyone in Lahoya who is able to farm, does so. Because of the tremendous variation in altitude in the sierra, the planting and harvesting cycle in Lahoya's agricultural lands strongly depends on the climate in a given zone. Three categories are generally recognized in this sense: hot, in the valleys; cool, in high altitudes; and temperate, between the former and the latter. Most of the Lahoyan lands are in the cool to temperate zones.

In the cool highlands, corn is planted around February or March and weeded for the first time around the beginning of April. The corn is then harvested toward the end of July. Four or five types of beans are commonly intercropped, or planted between the rows of corn, in order to maximize the use of land and labor.

In the temperate climate, sugarcane is planted around February or March. A common practice is to plant bananas along with the sugarcane because the former can be used to flavor the panela when it is processed. In the temperate zone, sugarcane can take two years to mature. It also needs to be weeded two or three times a year to ensure a robust and productive yield. Sometimes a second corn crop is planted in the temperate zone toward the end of October and harvested around February.

In addition, chiles, vegetables, coffee, pepper, and vanilla are planted in small quantities. Most of these crops are utilized primarily in domestic consumption, but surplus production can also be sold locally. According to Lahoyans in Mexico City who had left the village in the mid-1960s, the merchants and traders who came into the village were principally from the regional marketing center of Zoogocho, as well as the towns of Solaga and Yalalag. In contrast, Lahoyans could always walk over to the weekly market in Ralu'a if they wanted to sell surplus produce, but Ralu'an merchants did not generally come to Lahoya.

Up to 1980 (the last point at which I have data in this regard), the main agricultural technique of the Lahoyans was basically a kind of rotating slash-and-burn style. According to local practice, the brush where a field is to be planned is cut some two months before. Everything is allowed to dry, and then the field is burned, the land is lightly plowed, and the crops are planted. The practice is to cultivate different fields in the following years to allow the soil to lie fallow. The same cycle is then repeated when the land is deemed ready for cultivation again.

According to the national census taken by the Mexican government in 1970 (DGE 1973), the land base of the larger municipality of Lahoya was held in approximately 170 parcels, almost two-thirds of which were less than 5 hectares in size. The other third of the land, held in units greater than 5 hectares, represented half of all the arable land.[3] In contrast to other Mountain Zapotec villages, there is no communal land in Lahoya, and apparently there never has been. The closest thing that the village has to this are the *barrio* lands. The barrios of Lahoya are, in this case, nonterritorially based religious organizations (unlike barrio groups in other Mexican communities, in which membership is tied to location within a village).

In contrast to the style of agriculture in the neighboring Ralu'a, Lahoyan women and older children of both sexes actively participate in agricultural tasks along with the men. Also in contrast to the practice in Ralu'a, sons continue to work with their fathers after they become adults and even after marriage. Other arrangements are also possible. A father may give an unmarried son the opportunity to work by himself on a piece of the father's land, or the two can make an arrangement based on partnership and mutual aid. In any case, a father retains control over his property; sons must wait until their father's death to assume ownership of land.

Informants in Mexico City remembered the life of the 1950s and 1960s as routine and sparse. If they had the basic resources, such as land, seed, and tools, informants estimated that an average family could get by on about a thousand pesos (at the time, about eighty U.S. dollars) a year. If there was a need for cash to purchase other essentials such as cloth and shoes, surplus crops could be sold to traders from other regional market plazas, including San Miguel Cajonos and Zoogocho, or traded or sold in the market at Ralu'a. One bought new clothing during Semana Santa, or Holy Week, and these would have to last for the rest of the year. They were always plain, durable clothes; one doesn't need to dress up to work in the *campo*, I was told.

Lahoyan families generally go out to work in their fields for weeks at a time. In fact, most families reside outside of the community of Lahoya proper for most of the year, living dispersed in lean-tos out in their fields. Beyond this, migrants recalled that one worked, ate, and slept. There was little else to do and little in the way of entertainment.

Three additional points can be made about the general agricultural situation in Lahoya since 1970. First, while there is land enough for everyone who remains in the village, the best agricultural lands, and land within the immediate perimeter of Lahoya that is suitable for building on, seems to be concentrated in the hands of a small number of relatively well-off families. Second, wage laborers are simply not available. I was repeatedly told that Lahoyans do not sell wage labor to other villagers, and in fact the 1980 national census indicates that only 5 percent of the work force in the entire municipality sold wage labor for a living. This situation, along with the general absence of the kind of cooperative labor groups or labor exchange mechanisms found in neighboring villages, influences fathers and sons to combine forces even after the latter have married and established their own families. Third, the traditional conservative agricultural practices of the village were said by many outmigrants I spoke with to have resulted in a general state of agricultural stagnation. Few new plants or agricultural methods are adopted or employed, and production is oriented primarily toward self-provisionment. This claim is at least partially substantiated by the 1980 national census, which indicates that income levels are far below those of Ralu'a or Villa Alta.

Municipal Organization

Today, the municipality of Lahoya is made up of the village of Lahoya and a small *rancho* attached to the village. The civil authority in Lahoya is an elected municipal government that coordinates village activities and handles problems and conflicts. Despite slight variations, municipal offices and duties are similar to those of San Juan Juquila Vijanos (as described in Nader 1965).

Legal matters are handled in the municipal building, where three officials are in charge of village affairs. The first two are the village president and the *síndico* (the prosecutor of the village court), whose responsibilities are somewhat overlapping. The role of the president is essentially administrative; he takes care of matters such as fiestas, the police, and the adjudication of lesser cases. The síndico is in charge of the tequio and complaints involving fighting, gossip, land disputes, and witchcraft. A third municipal official, the *alcalde* (judge), is responsible for adjudicating domestic quarrels, deaths, and more serious crimes, which must often be reported to Villa Alta, the district seat. The municipal offices are open from 6 A.M. to 8 P.M. daily, although the cases that are actually brought in during the week are few in number.

As in other Mountain Zapotec villages, every male citizen between the ages of eighteen and sixty owes service to the municipal government. Civic service is given in two principal ways. First, every man must serve his share of posts in the municipal government. How high he goes in the hierarchy of positions is determined by both his social standing and his capacities. Second, every able-bodied man must provide his fair share of labor in the village *tequios*.[4]

Apart from the formal institutions and offices of the municipal government, the process of governance since the 1950s has been affected by a small group of families who can influence village affairs but cannot totally control them. Interviews suggest that some stratification developed after World War II as the wealthier families obtained some of the best lands in the immediate vicinity of the village. Their hold over the village also appears to be based on prestige (especially their higher educational levels) and on their connections to the outside world, for the heads of the important families have become brokers in the larger legal and political system linking Lahoya to the district seat.

Family and Social Organization

Turning to selected aspects of social organization, men in the village have tended to marry between the ages of eighteen and twenty, while women have tended to marry at a younger age, often between fourteen and seventeen years—twenty at the latest. If a woman reaches twenty-five years and is still unmarried, people begin to comment, "Ya pasó el tren" (literally, The train left [that one behind]) or "Na' más sirve para vestir santos" (She's only good for dressing saints; i.e., she will probably remain a spinster and devote herself to the Church). The youthful age at marriage again reflects both cultural values and the importance of the production strategy of self-provisioning agriculture, which requires the cooperative efforts of a nuclear or extended family. In 1950, for example, when the population of the larger municipality was at a high of 1,177, 85 percent of the households were nuclear families made up of either couples or parents and children (DGE 1954).[5] About 15 percent of the population was attached to a nuclear family-based household. Further, although some 230 persons were listed as single, less than 1 percent of the populace lived alone, which demonstrates the importance of the household as a basic unit of both production and consumption in a self-provisioning economy. Marriages in Lahoya, as throughout the Rincón, tend to be endogamous.

Since they generally live out in their fields while working, many families return to the village only for periods of rest or when they need to fulfill civic duties, religious observances, and so forth. These periods, which allow a respite from isolation and the rigors of daily labor, are also the richest socially and culturally, since children can play games with their peers, kin and friends can gather for a visit or a drink, and people can organize and celebrate village fiestas.

Lahoyans in Mexico City told me that the village is divided into two parts— Juárez and Hidalgo—representing the upper and lower halves of Lahoya, respectively. This is a territorially based distinction that does not involve kinship. Similar to the barrio, which characterizes the organization of Mexican peasant communities (Hunt and Nash 1967:260–68; although, again, barrios are the name for religious associations in the Rincón), one of the main cultural institutions of Lahoya, the village bands, was based on this division. Until the mid-1960s, that is, both the upper and the lower halves of the village had bands that coexisted in a spirit of friendly competition. Surprisingly, eligibility and membership in a band was not contingent on whether one actually resided in Juárez or Hidalgo. The bands may have reflected political divisions within the village (although not the division between progressives and conservatives that has been noted in neighboring Zapotec villages like Ralu'a).

Otherwise, although they do practice *gozona* on occasion, Lahoyans lack the many intravillage associations and multiple institutions of reciprocal exchange characteristic of neighboring Mountain Zapotec villages. In fact, one of the salient characteristics of the village is intravillage factionalism and conflict. The development of factions appears to have three overlapping and interacting bases. There has been feuding over plots of land, especially their boundaries. Some of this fighting has been due to personal animosities. Second, there has been conflict over competing sets of philosophical interests based on the opposition between private property and public need. For example, at one time the villagers wanted to build an elementary school on a privately owned lot that was conveniently located in the center of town, but the owner refused to give up his parcel. Villagers, especially parents, were furious, but the man proved to be intractable and even threatened to prosecute trespassers. Third, as will be explained in detail below, conflict between Lahoyan migrants in Mexico City and the village elites over the development process in Lahoya has generated major intracommunity divisions.

What is more, since informal village mechanisms for resolving grievances and disputes appear to be minimal, the escalation of community conflicts has been a frequent problem. As a result, some of the more intense village political battles have escalated all the way up to state and even federal offices, courts, and legislatures.

The family, then, is the primary unit of social organization in Lahoya, much as it is among the Zapotec as a whole. Beyond this, the social organization of Lahoya is largely formal in nature and revolves around activities in two interrelated areas of village life: civic and religious service.

Religion

The national census of 1980 reports that some 96 percent of the population in the municipality was Catholic. Religion in the village is based on a strong belief in the Catholic saints, and religious duties are taken very seriously. Vestiges of a *mayordomía* system, an institution with set positions and duties organized to care for and honor the saints, existed through the early 1970s. Celebrations have since been curtailed, apparently because of extensive outmigration.

According to informants, Lahoya's church houses a large collection of statues of saints, many of which are now antiques. Lahoyans believe that the saints can act as intermediaries between people and God; thus, one can pray to a specific saint for a cure for sickness, on behalf of one's children, or for a special wish. During the mayordomía, when the saints were honored they were taken from the church, paraded around the village, and might be placed for a period of time in individual homes. Beyond their spiritual significance, the religious festivals integral to the mayordomía were the main village-level cultural and economic events in which families and individuals participated collectively.[6]

Local Patterns of Development

The relative impoverishment of Lahoya's local development becomes clear when we examine traditional occupations; in fact, few occupations are available, nor are there local crafts outside of brewing homemade alcohol.[7] Only a few men have been able to amass enough capital to loan money or to engage in local commerce.

For those individuals or families seeking economic alternatives, four recourses have traditionally been available, all involving emigration from the village for short to long periods of time. One alternative, which has been practiced for years, is to seek work in the mining industry of the neighboring district of Ixtlán. Similarly, some have sought employment down in the *bajos*—that is, down toward the Gulf Coast of Veracruz north of Lahoya. Not many men have done this, but I was told that a good salary could be earned if one was willing to work as a wage laborer on sugarcane or banana plantations. More commonly, men and women could opt to sell wage labor in Ralu'a, especially during peak agricultural periods such as the coffee harvest. Finally, and increasingly since the 1950s, out-migration to Oaxaca City or Mexico City has become an attractive option for those who become discouraged with their lives or future prospects.

Development projects have been initiated in Lahoya through a combination of various sources of money and leadership: out-migrants, state and federal agencies and officials, and the local elite. A potable-water system was installed in 1965, and electricity became available in 1968. Even by 1979, however, there was no store in Lahoya, although soft drinks and liquor were sold at several houses. In short, there has been little development to speak of. The village hosts no agencies or government commissions, and thus no new jobs have been generated in this regard. A few men have managed to leave Lahoya in order to become primary-school teachers, most of whom work in schools outside of Villa Alta, but a few have returned to teach in the Sierra Juárez and even Lahoya itself.

Lahoya has access to postal and telegraphic service only via Ralu'a's services. Through tequio and government grants, a road was completed between Ralu'a and Lahoya in the early 1970s. Unfortunately, the work was so poorly executed that the road is not usable during the rainy season even by trucks. There is no landing strip in Lahoya, so the main means of transportation in and out of the village is by foot.

Conclusion

Perhaps resulting as much from its economic stagnation as anything else, Lahoya has the appearance of being a conservative Mountain Zapotec village. Zapotec remains the primary language, and vestiges of the traditional (albeit postconquest) religious *cargo* system are still in existence. Even by the 1980s, few Lahoyans were able to go beyond the first three years of primary school. Belief in witchcraft remained strong enough through the 1970s that formal charges could be presented before the village authorities if an individual believed he or she was being subjected to attack by a witch.[8] As late as the 1950s, even doing or having something that caused envy was believed to be enough to call witchcraft down upon oneself. Perhaps it is an atypical example, but one Lahoyan migrant told me that he remembered surreptitiously washing some meat off once in a stream near the village, aware that he should do his best to conceal it from his neighbors. Thus, cosmological beliefs create a climate of suspicion in the village. Within such a climate it is understandable, again, why multiple relationships of association and reciprocity might be limited even though they would be all the more important (see Kearney 1972 and Selby 1974).

On a more positive note, many Lahoyans I spoke with mentioned the village bands as a major source of culture and diversion. When someone wanted to join one of the bands, they arranged to study with the director, who provided basic musical instruction. Each candidate had to purchase his own instrument from Oaxaca City, which entailed a considerable expense. Training lasted up to half a year, and after this the individual was eligible to join. The bands did not practice on a regular basis. Rather, musicians got together two or three weeks before a major fiesta to work on their repertoire. The bands had a room (called the *escoleta* locally) where they could practice, as well as socialize as a group, away from their families. Similar to the Lahoyan migrants, many of the Mountain Zapotec who had played music in such bands and who continued this interest in Mexico City emphasized that the sentiment expressed in the music of the sierra was one of its most important qualities and that a band's music is part of the soul of the Mountain Zapotec villages.[9]

In summary, Lahoya is the poorest and seemingly one of the most conservative villages in the periphery of Ralu'a. Serranos, including the Lahoyans, recognize this fact, and to some extent it creates a sense of stigmatization, affecting Lahoyans' self-perceptions and interaction. As we will see, these perceptions are brought to Mexico City and affect the relationships among

Lahoyans themselves, between Lahoyans and out-migrants from surrounding villages, and with residents of Mexico City in general.

RALU'A: THE REGIONAL MARKETING CENTER

Although Ralu'a was a town of only 2,000 people when I first visited it in 1975, it was the largest community in the area, and its residents had built a landing strip at the edge of the community big enough for a single-engine plane to land. It takes about forty-five minutes to fly to Ralu'a from the airport in Oaxaca City. The view is fantastic. The mountains gradually spring up on the edges of the Valley of Oaxaca and then grow larger and larger as if they were a series of waves washing up on a beach. In the space of only a few minutes' travel, there may be several great climbs and drops in altitude, from a river or a valley to a mountaintop and then back down to a valley again. If one goes in the summer months, as I did, there are myriad shades of green on the slopes of the sierra, and it is surprising how much of the area is or has been used for crops. Fields that are literally hanging on the sides of great mountains have been cut and burned clear, and there a farmer has his plot and *jacal* (hut).

Ralu'a is known locally as a new, that is, postconquest, settlement. Ralu'a's location among preconquest communities has traditionally made its territorial base precarious, and its limited agricultural lands may have influenced the town's orientation toward cash crops and commerce (Nader 1964). In spite of this background, in the sense that its residents have striven to overcome constraints that derive from a fixed and limited land base, both the town and the larger municipality have had a fairly consistent pattern of growth since 1940, especially when taking out-migration into account. Ralu'a, for example, had a population of 1,622 in 1940, which grew by 140 persons by the end of the following decade and to more than 2,000 persons by 1960. The population remained at about 2,000 through the 1970s and continued to grow during the 1980s. Two conditions must be taken into account when considering this pattern of growth: first, health and hygienic standards have greatly improved since the 1950s, and thus infant mortality rates have dropped; second, there has been a great deal of in-migration from the self-provisioning agricultural villages in the hinterlands surrounding Ralu'a. These two trends have almost completely offset the decline in population because of the extensive out-migration from the town.

Economic Base

Although its economy is quite diversified, as we will soon see, agriculture remains central to the economic base of Ralu'a. More than two-thirds of the arable landholdings in Ralu'a are small (i.e., less than five hectares in size), and a landowner's property is often fragmented due to the limited amount of arable land and the custom of providing an equal inheritance to all children. Crops include corn, beans, sugarcane, and various vegetables and fruits that are consumed primarily by the farmer's own family. Since the 1930s coffee has been a major cash crop.[10] As a result, the production of subsistence crops in Ralu'a has been reduced to about 40 percent of the total agricultural output. A road suitable for motor vehicles was completed in 1959, but the remoteness of the town and the difficulty of transporting products out of the region limited the efficient sale and marketing of cash crops through the 1970s.

Since the mines closed in the early 1900s, the town has had no local industry to speak of. Men and women can pursue a large number of crafts and traditional occupations, but only rarely can enough money be earned at these to allow people to abandon agriculture altogether. Craft occupations for men include being blacksmiths, barbers, bakers, carpenters and builders, and butchers, or they involve skills like working leather, producing fireworks, or making and selling liquor. Some crafts require little in the way of tools and expense, while others demand more capital outlay, specialized tools, and skills, and so are not feasible alternatives for everyone.

Women, too, have many traditional crafts they can pursue for part-time supplementary work, including sewing (but not weaving), animal husbandry, washing, making and selling food, tortillas, and gathering and selling firewood. A few women are servants. Women may also sell wage labor during key periods of the agricultural cycle. The coffee harvest, which runs from January through March, is a time when women's labor is most in demand and most highly paid (Young 1982). Those with the knowledge and skill may serve as midwives or as curers, but the demand for such services may decline because the government established a municipal health center in Ralu'a in the late 1970s.

While many Ralu'an families value local crafts and find pleasure in the creativity and autonomy that self-provisionment can entail, what a given household is unable or unwilling to produce for itself is usually available at the weekly Ralu'an market. Since distances are difficult to negotiate, and regional variations encourage specialization in resources and crafts, a weekly market cycle has long been established in the region (Beals 1971; Berg 1974). Goods range from surplus agricultural produce to items of everyday utility (such as tools, shoes, clothing, liquor, and foodstuffs) and to more expensive manufactured items. In addition to the Ralu'an market, six or seven stores in the town are open on a daily basis. Three of these are quite large and extensively stocked. Not surprisingly, the wealthiest store owners head up the richest families in Ralu'a.

Ralu'a also has two bars and a number of smaller cantinas. The liquor sold there includes alcoholic beverages, such as *mescal* (cactus based), *aguar-*

diente (sugarcane based), *anís* (licorice) liquor, and *tepache* (a local fermented drink made of panela and *pulque,* a beer brewed from cactus), as well as the more expensive bottled beers and distilled liquors from Oaxaca City. Moderate indulgence is an occasional pleasant pastime for men (women, if and when they do drink, do not usually drink in public). Excessive drinking, however, is frowned upon, and heavy drinkers—typically men—experience pressure to stop from their wives, parents, family, and even the municipal authorities.

Ralu'a basically operates within a monetized economy due to the degree of commercial development in the town and the fact that it is the main market center for the immediate area. Trade and credit can still be arranged on a nonmonetary basis, but even these arrangements are based on peso values as a standard equivalent. In fact, the members of every household in Ralu'a have to have some cash income insofar as they consume electricity or have piped water in their homes.

Social Stratification

Turning to the topic of social stratification, there is definitely class distinction among farmers based on the quality and size of their holdings, although even as late as the 1970s wealthy men with good land who could afford to hire a number of laborers usually worked side by side in the fields with them if they were physically able to do so. In short, while stratification is present in Ralu'a, and is certainly more developed than in communities like Lahoya, its manifestations are more subtle and less invidious than those that characteristically appear in urban settings like Oaxaca or Mexico City. Perhaps class differences are most invidious for those who are desperately poor.

As a partial index of stratification, merchants in Ralu'a and people who have substantial savings are sometimes willing to lend money, but I heard comments both in the town and in Mexico City that exorbitant interest rates are sometimes charged for this "favor." One man, for example, told me that even borrowing money was difficult. No one will lend money without collateral, and foreclosure on land offered as collateral was one of the main ways that the poorer families lost what little property they had. Another system of providing collateral for a loan involves giving the lender the right to reap the coffee crop on a given plot for, say, five years in a row. This is why many residents prefer to borrow from the barrio association if they can, because the latter charges only about 20 percent annual interest.

According to an economic survey carried out by anthropologist Kate Young in 1975, some 20 percent of the community's families were considered "wealthy" by local standards—that is, they could consistently hire wage labor to work in their fields.[11] Other traits and conditions accompanied this status. These families generally had the best and largest landholdings. Also, many of these same families originally supported building a road and, once it was complete, initiated transportation services between Ralu'a and Oaxaca City that they later used as a base for additional commercial and entrepreneurial activities. These families were thus in the best position to generate surplus capital from agriculture and could use the profits to set up stores. A number of wealthy families, however, simply produced and sold coffee.

About 40 percent of the households in Ralu'a were in the middle—that is, they were prosperous enough to hire laborers on occasion. The other 40 percent of Ralu'a's households had enough land to grow subsistence crops but also had to find ways to supplement their income, usually through wage labor or the practice of a traditional craft.

Largely as a result of Ralu'a's labor shortage, along with the lack of work in many of the neighboring villages, a growing "colony" of settlers has been created among people who have migrated to Ralu'a from surrounding villages to sell wage labor. Many of these settlers are given "citizenship" in the town (and sometimes a small plot of land at the upper edge of the town on which to build their houses) once they have established their willingness to participate in tequio and serve in the municipal government. By the mid-1970s these settlers constituted a new level in the system of socioeconomic stratification in Ralu'a: landless people who were thus more-or-less permanently agricultural wage-laborers.[12]

The changes in the economy and in patterns of consumption described above have brought increasing stratification to Ralu'a, but although the control exerted by the wealthy families is strong, they do not constitute an aristocracy. Ralu'ans in both Oaxaca and in Mexico City insisted that, since the government is popularly elected and depends on cooperation in order to function, there are no real *caciques* (political bosses) in Ralu'a.

From 1950 through the 1980s the town of Ralu'a was thus a steadily growing community that also acted as a municipal center encompassing a number of smaller villages and dependencies. Ralu'a manifests increasing signs of socioeconomic stratification although a popularly elected municipal government runs the town and manages the affairs of the larger municipal entity (Nader 1964, 1990).

Family and Social Organization

Turning to selected features of social organization, one of the most important units of Ralu'an community life is the nuclear family. As in Lahoya, the main reason has to do with the economic role of the family as "the largest production and consumption unit." Because there are more varied economic opportunities than in Lahoya, however, it appears that more people in Ralu'a can opt to live alone (DGE 1954). Marriage patterns are endogamous by preference, but because of a more open attitude toward "outsiders," marriages between Ralu'ans and people from other Mountain Zapotec communities are accepted.

Again, as in Lahoya, the nuclear family is the ideal in Ralu'a; even if two or more nuclear families are under the same roof, they tend to cook separately. Often, in practice, nuclear families have additional members, but recruitment to a household is typically based on a kinship tie (DGE 1954). Families, especially children, are valued in their own right in Ralu'a, and as we will see later, the desire to maximize opportunities for their children constituted a major motive for Ralu'ans to leave the village in the 1970s.

At a broader level, a central aspect of the social organization of Ralu'a centers around work groups beyond those at the nuclear family level, because some jobs—such as house building, roof repairing, harvesting, and conducting funerals—are more quickly and efficiently carried out with a larger group on hand. The *gozona,* or mutual aid group, is formed on the basis of labor exchange over the long term.[13] In gozona, food and drink are provided by the host, a record is kept of participation, and reciprocity is required. If a man is not able to attend a gozona in person, he is obliged to hire a worker to take his place. Work in partnership (*en compañía*) is mostly used for smaller tasks of agricultural labor. On the other hand, if a man has enough money, he may hire laborers (*mozos*) to work his fields. This is a strictly cash arrangement between a *patrón* and the men or women he hires.

Turning to an overview of formal associations and organizations, Ralu'a has barrios (as noted above, these are not the well-known territorial divisions frequently found in Mexican villages but nonterritorial groups with religious, economic, and tax functions); neighborhood associations, which have similar economic and religious functions but which are formed mainly by women on a neighborhood basis; church organizations, almost like corporate groups in that they hold collective property; a town band and orchestra; communal work groups; and formal associations that administer the town's wells and the chapels (Nader 1964:236–42). What is striking about these formal groupings is their number and the fact that they are based on principles of mutual aid and cooperation.

Mutual aid also appears in the informal associations that occur during the daily round of activities. If men work in contiguous fields, they may interact or eat their meals with each other. In Ralu'a, when work is done, afternoons and evenings are a time for informal association with relatives, neighbors, and friends. Men may go to the cantina for a drink. Women find ample opportunities for conviviality when taking corn to the *nixtamal* to be ground, doing the wash, and going to church. For both men and women, market day is a time for socializing and visiting. Saint's days, weddings, and funerals are special events that bring families and friends together.

An important aspect of the social organization of Ralu'a has been described in terms of cross-cutting ties that integrate the different levels and groupings within the town (Nader 1964), but cross-linkages can have both positive and negative effects. On the positive side, they can provide cohesion in neighborhood settings where relatives and nonrelatives are tightly clustered together. On the negative side, such cohesion may actually weaken the ties within nuclear families (Nader 1964:251).

The History of the Road

Before 1960, transportation and travel between Oaxaca City and Ralu'a was slow and difficult. The bulk of the coffee that left the sector, for example, had to be carried out by animal (or even human) transport to the nearest market center in the district that had access to a paved road. After many years of sacrifice and struggle, a functional road into Ralu'a was finally completed in 1959. The road allowed direct transportation to and from the town, and Ralu'a became the dominant commercial center in the region (Berg 1974:58).

Because of its tremendous regional impact, the history of the road into Ralu'a is worth considering at length. Work on the road was initiated with great enthusiasm around 1925. Drawing primarily from the tequio labor of just one community was insufficient, so Ralu'a invited neighboring communities to participate. Some of them actually did send work parties, but others roundly refused. Work continued in this fashion for some time but was then suspended until 1940.

From 1940 to 1943, various expeditions were launched from Ralu'a in order to chart the best course for the road through the rugged sierra. Nothing came of any plans until 1949 because of the tremendous challenges that completing a passable road through this terrain presented. The committee that the municipal authorities formed to support the construction of the road was composed of six men in their thirties—men who would, incidentally, become some of the most influential leaders of Ralu'a by the mid-1970s. These men organized the Ralu'ans into special work teams, but the committee soon realized that although they had the will and the manpower to build the road, they lacked the technical expertise to implement the project. They decided to approach the state government of Oaxaca to ask for assistance.

The committee was warmly received in Oaxaca by the state governor, Don Eduardo Vasconcelos. Sympathetic to the petition of the Ralu'ans, Governor Vasconcelos appointed a special commission to investigate the situation. It was made up of distinguished members of his government—men such as Sr. Fidencio Hernández, a member of the Justice Department, and Professor José L. Tamayo, an eminent Mexican geographer. Unfortunately, despite great efforts to advance the road before commission members arrived to inspect the work, Hernández informed the Ralu'ans that the project should be suspended because the government simply could not afford to underwrite construction at that time. The next month, however, an engineer was sent by the state to study possible routes, which encouraged the committee and the villagers very much. By March 1949, under the supervision of the engineer, work was initiated once again on the basis of tequio labor.

Progress on the road was so slow and discouraging that work again became intermittent. Over the next year the president of Ralu'a made more than twenty trips to Oaxaca City to petition for state aid. Finally, perhaps seeing the village's enthusiasm and the tremendous sacrifices that were being made, state officials promised to grant 2,500 pesos for each kilometer of road completed. The federal government, then headed by President Miguel Alemán, also agreed to provide 2,500 pesos per kilometer under the auspices of the Department of Communications and Public Works. The catch was that all of the villages in the immediate area had to provide tequio labor for the project, a requirement that many villages were not inclined to fulfill. Nevertheless, work was renewed on this basis between 1951 and 1952. Costs were so high, however, that the committee had to appeal to the wealthier families of Ralu'a to make individual donations to support the road work. Appeals were also made to all Ralu'ans living in other parts of the republic, especially in Mexico City, and the majority of them contributed as much as they were able. More money was needed, however, and the municipal authorities of Ralu'a were soon petitioning state and federal officials anew for additional support.

In 1953 Ralu'a gained a major victory. With the help of Professor Tamayo, a deal was struck which brought an additional 525,000 pesos to the project, a sum that was raised among the Papaloapan Commission, the Department of Local Communications (Comunicaciones Vecinales), and the state of Oaxaca. For its part, Ralu'a was responsible for generating an additional 90,000 pesos, so appeals were made to all the Ralu'ans living in Mexico City and in other cities for additional "cooperation." No efforts were spared, and over the next six years, two different construction companies, hundreds of men from the Rincón who gave their labor for free, and hired laborers worked together to complete the road.

On October 27, 1959, after thirty-four years of struggle, the first wheeled vehicle to pass over the entire new road arrived in Ralu'a. A huge public celebration was organized by the Ralu'an municipal authorities to celebrate the culmination of years of effort and work.

Because the road was rough—suitable principally for heavy transport trucks, or at least vehicles with four-wheel drive—a small commercial air service was established in Oaxaca City during the 1960s that served the sierra and points north into Veracruz. Ralu'a was one of the first villages to complete its landing strip, in 1963. Weather permitting, the planes landed several times during the week. By the 1960s, then, when both the road and the landing strip were completed, travel between the town and Oaxaca City became a reality. It is true that the fourteen- to twenty-hour trip in the back of a large cargo truck was difficult (and passengers often had to stand up in the back in all kinds of weather), but prices were low. By the middle of the 1960s, these trucks were making the trip back and forth from Oaxaca City several times a week. Between 1975 and 1979, additional work was carried out on the road, improving it to the point that a bus service between Ralu'a and Oaxaca City was initiated in the early 1980s.

Local Patterns of Development

As a leading municipal center, Ralu'a has experienced a sustained pattern of growth and development during the twentieth century. The town had the first primary school in the immediate area (established in 1910), and mail service and a telegraph service were opened shortly thereafter.

New occupations in Ralu'a have increased slowly since the 1960s, growing in proportion to the town's integration with the state and the nation. An electrical commission, the expansion of postal and transportation services, government agencies such as CONASUPO (which sold foodstuffs at subsidized prices) and INMECAFE (the Mexican government's coffee institute), and the town's schools are all sources of employment for a small number of local men. The fortunate few who obtain good jobs can often leave the fields, learn new skills, and make a decent income. Certainly the principal coffee growers, brokers, and local merchants have benefited disproportionately from the changes that have occurred since World War II. In contrast, beyond enjoying an increased demand for basic services, very few adult women have benefited occupationally from any of these recent changes.

In summary, change in Ralu'a has largely been the result of contacts with the outside world, contacts that the Ralu'ans themselves sometimes sought (Nader 1964). Concomitantly, Ralu'a has the reputation of being one of the most progressive villages in the district. The Ralu'ans themselves are quite aware, and proud, of this reputation. For this reason, and because of strong loyalties, sometimes Ralu'ans are critical of Zapotecs from neighboring villages. Nevertheless, although by the late 1970s only the oldest inhabitants and those newly arrived from the neighboring villages were monolingual speakers of Zapotec, Ralu'ans continue to see themselves as locals, and thus ultimately as Zapotec and as natives of the region.[14]

Conclusion

Although the town's economy is still based on agriculture, Ralu'ans have emphasized cash cropping to a much greater extent than people in the surrounding communities. The Ralu'an economy by the 1970s was thus the most strongly integrated with the outside world and also the most diversified in the Rincón. The town is also the location of many government offices that serve Ralu'a and surrounding municipalities.

At the same time that Ralu'a's economy diversified and grew, there is some indication that there was a labor shortage in the village during the mid to late 1970s. About half of the households in the town sold wage labor at some point during the year, but Ralu'ans commented on the scarcity of wage labor even though the wages offered for such work were considered to be very good. The influx of Zapotecs from the surrounding villages has been an important resource for Ralu'an farmers, and in-migrants also helped to minimize the net population loss as hundreds of Ralu'ans sought opportunities in Oaxaca and especially Mexico City in the 1960s and 1970s.

VILLA ALTA: THE DISTRICT SEAT

Villa Alta is a postconquest Spanish settlement established in the sixteenth century as the administrative center for the district. Villa Alta also served as a regional marketing center (Chance 1989). As a result of such origins, Spanish is the primary language spoken in Villa Alta, and residents have traditionally been regarded as Spanish (de la Fuente 1965). This has undergone change over the course of the twentieth century because there has been a significant pattern of both out-migration of residents to Oaxaca and Mexico City and in-migration of Zapotecs from surrounding villages. Today, Villaltecos are more properly seen as a mestizo population. For a time, the town of Villa Alta experienced a fairly consistent pattern of growth, increasing from 676 residents in 1940 to 914 in 1970. Since 1970, however, there has been a fairly dramatic population decline to a low of 572 residents in 1984 (Parnell 1988:3), with in-migration from surrounding communities not really offsetting out-migration.

Accounts by Parnell (1988) and Chance (1989) delineate Villa Alta's historical and contemporary function as an administrative center. The fact that it is the seat of local representatives of the state and national governments has served to channel power and wealth into the town from the villages in the hinterlands.[15] Administrative power within the district exists in combination with mercantile interests such as credit financing and the brokerage of cash crops. Not surprisingly, the 1980 national census indicates that the residents of the municipal district of Villa Alta have a much higher median income than the residents of Lahoya or even Ralu'a.

Political Dynamics

Unfortunately, published census data do not provide useful information concerning the town of Villa Alta. The data, that is, aggregate information pertaining to a number of settlements attached to Villa Alta that are oriented to self-provisioning agriculture. Nonetheless, it can be said that Villa Alta remains the district's administrative and mercantile center. According to Parnell, despite this fact, and despite its status as the district seat, civil *cargos*, tequio duties, and vestiges of the mayordomía—customs that might otherwise be ascribed to an indigenous peasant tradition—are still practiced in Villa Alta (Parnell 1988:chaps. 2–3). These communal traditions exist simultaneously with political bossism and provide the two key ways that Villalteco men gain prestige and power (Parnell 1988:39).

Since the 1950s, the political and social dynamics of Villa Alta have been dominated by a division between competing factions of bosses and their followers. On one side are the Caleros (the followers of Juan Calero), whose programs revolve around two key principles: to minimize the importance of village development projects (and accompanying and associated burdens such as quotas, tequios, and the town's government bureaucracy), and to maximize the input of local representatives and supporters of the Catholic Church vis-à-vis village life and governance (Parnell 1988:47).

Opposed to the Caleros are the Progressives, who are affiliated with the chief political boss (the *mero cacique*) of Villa Alta, David Mendiolea. A local businessman who often resides in Oaxaca City, Mendiolea and his followers have championed the use of government development programs to further the progress of Villa Alta. Specifically, their contributions involve bringing electricity and potable water to the village, repairing the Catholic church, constructing a new municipal building and offices, building secondary and technical schools, and bringing a rough road into the town from the neighboring community of Yalalag (Parnell 1988:44). One example, having to do with the construction of a new market place structure in the town, is described by Parnell as follows:

> Espinosa [the president of Villa Alta in 1983 and a member of the Mendiolea faction] initiated [the] project with state and federal funds and the cooperation of Progressive caciques to build a new market in the central square. He was to direct its construction in Villa Alta while Mendiolea provided communication and negotiation with government agencies in the capital. (Parnell 1988:49)

As Parnell points out, this project generated a number of paid positions for day laborers. In this fashion, funds obtained from the government through the efforts of Mendiolea and his followers could be used by the town's president to employ Villaltecos, and the town as a whole benefited because it gained a new building.

Eventually the Caleros—who generally opposed such projects, ostensibly because they create onerous burdens that have to be assumed by citizens of Villa Alta—could not remain idle in the face of the challenge that new public works represented to their status. According to Parnell, the Caleros' contribution was to construct a new road since the old road was not totally functional. The new one-lane dirt road, federally funded and maintained, ran through the district of Zacatepec. Unlike the old road, it passed through few of the Villa Alta district villages that in the past have contested the authority of the district seat and its residents (Parnell 1988:48).

Because they are cognizant of the fact that internal divisions could weaken social solidarity within the community as a whole, however, the citizens of Villa Alta are careful not to let factionalism get out of hand. This is accomplished in part by emphasizing a primary ethic that guides Villa Alta's relations to the outside world, namely, to maximize the overall strength and self-determination of Villa Alta vis-à-vis all external threats. This general rule, it might be added, holds whether the threat is exogenous (in the form of Protestant evangelists or agencies of the state, for example), or endogenous (such as the various regional assemblies of the sierra) (Parnell 1988:71 and passim). By 1984, when Parnell left the field, "the political groups of the divided district seat were locked as more or less equal opponents in dispute over principles of governance and the nature of village boundaries" (Parnell 1988:50).

Assuredly, the situation continues to evolve, both because of the regional politics Parnell described and because out-migration has been a significant demographic characteristic of the town since the 1960s and especially between 1970 and 1990. When compared to official Mexican census data for 1960 and 1970, Parnell's population estimate of 572 residents in 1984 suggests that out-migration from the district seat was as high as that of any other community in the district (Parnell 1988:3).

In the next chapter we will see that, as much as they reflected possible political difficulties that faced Villaltecos internally and externally, high rates of out-migration reflected special sets of occupational opportunities and personal connections that residents could access and use as a basis for geographic mobility and urban employment.

CONCLUSION

One way to view Lahoya, Ralu'a, and Villa Alta is in terms of a set of ideal types. These types illustrate the impact of local rural development processes on communities framed within a hierarchy of sociocultural integration. This can best be shown by comparing Mexican national census data summarizing the social, educational, and economic characteristics of the municipalities of the local marketing center and the district seat with those of predominantly self-sustaining agricultural communities in their hinterlands, such as Lahoya and its dependencies.

Since the sixteenth century, Villa Alta has been the administrative and financial center of the district. Ralu'a has had a steady pattern of growth and development, and it took off after 1960, when the entrance of the road made it the economic center of the region. By the 1970s, the towns of Villa Alta and Ralu'a were clearly the economic, and to a large extent the political and cultural, centers of this part of the sierra.

In social composition, 1980 census data suggest that the municipalities of both Villa Alta and Ralu'a are more heterogeneous than that of Lahoya. Both of the former have more persons born outside the communities. They also have more Protestants: 4 percent of Ralu'a's inhabitants were identified as such in 1980, and during the 1980s there was reputedly a dramatic increase in the number of Ralu'an Protestants. Similarly, more than 13 percent of Villa Alta's population was Protestant in 1980. By contrast, in 1980 only 1 percent of the inhabitants of the municipality of Lahoya had been born elsewhere and only 2 percent were Protestant (INEGI 1984).

Beyond this, how did local development influence the quality of life in the administrative and marketing centers compared to the outlying agricultural communities? One measure involves comparing language and educational levels in the larger municipalities of Ralu'a and Lahoya. Ralu'a had only a small proportion of monolingual Zapotec speakers after 1950 (10 percent by 1980), while more than one-quarter of the Lahoyan population was monolingual Zapotec in 1970 and 1980 (DGE 1973; INEGI 1984). On the question of literacy, in 1970 only one-fifth of the municipal residents of Ralu'a and Villa Alta were illiterate, but almost a third of the Lahoyan municipal residents could neither read nor write. Gender is a consideration here, however. It is significant that, irrespective of whether they lived in Villa Alta, Ralu'a, or Lahoya, women were almost twice as likely to be illiterate as men. The data are not broken down by age, so I cannot be certain, but I would estimate, based on firsthand observation, that in Ralu'a such a gender differential levels out among the younger generation, especially among those born in the community, because both boys and girls are now sent to primary school.

The changing criteria for measuring education, as well as gaps in the census data over time, make assessment of the general educational achievements of each municipality's residents somewhat inconclusive. The fact remains, however, that approximately one-third of the residents of the *municipios* of Ralu'a and Villa Alta had completed more than a primary education by 1970. By comparison, since the school in Lahoya includes only the first three grades out of an official six-year primary-school curriculum, only 4 percent of the Lahoyans had been able to complete or go beyond six years of education.

Next consider occupations and the structure of the labor force of the three municipalities. A comparison of the data for Ralu'a and Lahoya in 1960 provides a clear picture of the differential impact of regional hierarchy and development. Work in Lahoya and Ralu'a revolves around agriculture. In 1960, however, the town of Ralu'a had 163 persons in occupations outside of agriculture. Lahoya had only six. Although an improvement in this area is suggested by the figures reported in the 1970 census, interviews with migrants who had recently visited Lahoya indicated that little had changed. By way of comparison, the 1980 national census specifies that approximately 95 percent of all employed people in the municipio of Lahoya still worked in the agricultural sector. Further, according to the data issued by the national census bureau in 1980, Villa Alta had almost 50 percent of its labor force working in occupations tied to light manufacturing, business, services, or "administration."

Naturally, these characteristics correlate closely with the income levels in each municipality according to the 1980 census. While the residents of Lahoya and its dependencies earned an average of between 1 and 590 pesos a month (in terms of the interval categories used by the Mexican census), the comparable monthly income of Ralu'ans and people in their affiliated communities ranged from 591 to 1,080 pesos. The average monthly income of those residing in Villa Alta was anywhere from three to six times that found in Lahoya, ranging from 1,971 to 3,610 pesos.

A final point of a more specifically ethnographic nature is the extent to which traditions and institutions of formal and informal mutual aid exist in each village. In general, customs involving mutual aid seem to be more prevalent in Ralu'a than in either Villa Alta or Lahoya, lending support to Long and Roberts's (1978) hypothesis that articulation with capitalist economic systems may actually reinforce "pre-capitalist" forms of mutual aid. Even though there is probably less mutual aid and fewer partnerships *en compañía* than in the past (Young 1978a), cooperative work groups are still used in Ralu'a for a wide range of household and civic tasks. By comparison, four factors help to explain the paucity of mutual aid practices in Lahoya apart from duties related to Catholicism or the municipal government. In Lahoya there was (1) a labor unit based on the self-provisioning nuclear family, (2) a more decentralized system of political organization than in Ralu'a or Villa Alta, (3) a tradition of witchcraft beliefs and practices, and (4) a history of factionalism and conflict in the village.

CHAPTER 5

Patterns of Out-Migration

This chapter focuses on migration from Lahoya and Ralu'a, including rural conditions influencing out-migration, migrant selectivity (considered in general, nonquantitative terms), the stated reasons for migration, and urban points of destination. The presentation relies on two key points: first, there were important differences between an early and a later period of out-migration, and second, different socioeconomic strata within the rural population were inclined to leave during each period, in accordance with conditions in the points of origin and destination. Here, as in the previous chapter, the emphasis is on the rural point of origin, recognizing that this is a largely analytical division, since conditions in both the point of origin and destination must be considered to obtain a complete picture.

OUT-MIGRATION FROM LAHOYA

Hard Times, 1940–1959

The first major stage of out-migration began during the decade of the 1940s and lasted until the late 1950s. Economic change set the stage for the initial period of out-migration inasmuch as the decline of a flourishing local market for panela depressed the village economy. Interviews also suggest that in the period before 1960 increasing pressure was being put on limited agricultural lands.

Out-migration from Lahoya began with a very small number of men who left the district during the 1940s. Among this group were less than ten braceros, who went to the United States. While some of these men did save their money and return to the village, informants agree that they had little economic or cultural impact back home (unlike the case described in Berg 1974:221–28). Within a few years, all the returnees had spent their money and were farming again just like everyone else.

It is difficult to determine the selectivity of migrants during this period.[1] Based on the information available, it seems that the bulk of the migrants were men and women who were young and single when they left Lahoya. Probably more women than men migrated from the village. In a number of cases, parents actually sent their children out. Some had higher aspirations for their children; others did so for economic necessity. Regarding the latter, for example, Sra. Bravo explained that her father had died when she was quite young. After that, even though they had some land, the family started having serious financial problems, so she left the village in 1942 at the age of eighteen. She went down to Oaxaca City—a trip that took four days by foot. She went with a paisana who was already working in Oaxaca and who helped her find a job.

Among the motivations for migrating that Lahoyans expressed, two themes were common. First, people talked about the backbreaking labor necessary in most aspects of daily life. Second, many people talked about an interrelated set of aspirations, which included the desire to learn Spanish and to continue their education. Somewhat to my surprise, none of the early migrants specifically mentioned difficulty in obtaining land as a motive for leaving Lahoya. Although little money was available in the village and there was little in the way of cultural life or entertainment beyond the major religious celebrations, migrants agreed that everyone was accustomed to such conditions. Certainly by general agreement of both early and later migrants, Lahoyans were not starving and thus did not flee the village out of dire necessity.

Between 1950—when out-migration from the district began to involve more than just a few persons—and 1957, most of the migrants from Lahoya went directly to Oaxaca City. Lahoyans reported that there were so many villagers there by the late 1950s that it was possible to arrive in Oaxaca City and get temporary lodging without any advance consultation or notice.

Because of the proximity of the state capital to Lahoya, continuing ties developed that played an important role in stimulating further out-migration. One of these involved visits or vacations taken by out-migrants who returned to Lahoya with stories of life in Oaxaca City. Not only did this create images in the minds of the villagers, who would inevitably compare stories about conditions in Oaxaca with those in Lahoya. It also provided a new alternative to those whose situations were, or became, difficult in the village: they could opt to leave with some hope of finding a tolerable future in Oaxaca City.

A Growing Exodus, 1960–1980s

A second stage of out-migration developed in the decade of the 1960s and lasted into the 1980s. In examining general conditions in Lahoya, it appears that nothing changed in its patterns of subsistence agriculture or the village economy as a whole. If anything, it became easier during this period to obtain land for farming because more people were leaving the village than were being born there or were migrating in. The only other factors that pertain here are a growing awareness of the conditions and lifestyle in the state capital and the Federal District, including a growing number of Lahoyans in Mexico City, and increasing factionalization and conflict in the village.

During this period, the backgrounds and characteristics of out-migrants diversified. While young, single migrants continued to predominate, their siblings were often able to join them, and sometimes even their parents. More men who were already married and had a family began to migrate. Older persons left as well, looking for easier ways to sustain themselves once they were past their prime.

An outstanding feature of both periods of migration from Lahoya is the large number of single women who left the village. Women from Lahoya who work in Mexico City as maids typically came to the city with compatriots. Lahoyans in Mexico City explained the situation as follows. Girls in the village saw a paisana from the capital at a fiesta or on a visit back home and, usually on the basis of economic need, requested that she take them to the city to work. Young women from Lahoya arrived in the capital fresh from the village in this fashion. They usually didn't speak Spanish and sometimes got confused or even lost in the vast urban agglomeration. During the later 1970s, these women could earn from 1,500 to 2,000 pesos a month if they were well trained. The Lahoyan maids generally "live in"; that is, they have their own room, are given their meals, and have one day a week off, often Sunday. Some, however, prefer to work by day and return to their own homes at night. I was told that no woman in particular, or group of women, is known for helping paisanas to get work as maids. Apparently the work is so basic and easy to find that many women have brought paisanas from the village and then helped to train them.

One interview with a maid stands out in my mind because it was the only time that I spoke at length with a Lahoyan women of approximately my own age (twenty-six at the time). I met Señorita Martínez at a small party one Saturday afternoon in Mexico City. She seemed willing to talk about her experience, so we sat off to the side and I was able to interview her at some length.

She told me she had left Lahoya in 1968. Her parents had split up and she did not get along with her stepfather very well. She also pointed out that work in Lahoya is heavy because, from about the age of twelve, women labor alongside the men: in addition to cooking and keeping house, women weed, harvest, and generally engage in heavy and difficult tasks in the fields. Señorita Martínez said that, like other young girls in Lahoya, it really made an impression on her when paisanas came back from Mexico City for a visit and she heard them talking about their life there. She said that this experience gives many back in the village the incentive (*ánima*) to give it a try themselves.

As a young teen, with her mother's permission, Señorita Martínez went with a paisana to Oaxaca City. The paisana helped her find work as a maid and showed her the ropes. She explained that the seasoned migrants would tell the neophyte how a maid needed to dress, how to act, and generally what to do. She also emphasized that since every employer had her own way of cleaning and arranging things around the home, a maid needed to be sensitive to the señora of the house in order to respond satisfactorily.

Eventually, Señorita Martínez decided to go to Mexico City. She did not have anything lined up but said that since it was much easier for a woman to find a job than a man, she wasn't worried about it. She had to work in a couple of different homes in the beginning but had been at her present place of employment for six years. She works there as a live-in maid, likes her employers, and told me that she earned around a 1,000 pesos a month (which in retrospect seems understated). She was happy she hadn't had to move around and vastly preferred working in the same place. She said that she was not lonely, as she knows and is known by everyone in the apartment building. If an emergency comes up, she added, she had friends in the building who would help her out.

When I asked if the move as a whole was for the better, she responded by saying that being a maid basically involved work that women in Lahoya have to do anyhow. By comparison, life in the capital was much lighter because the pay and conditions were so much better than those available in the village. Like Señorita Martínez, many of the young Lahoyan women apparently migrated because they had few alternatives besides a life of strenuous labor in the fields.

Turning now to other stated motives for migration in the 1960s and 1970s, four themes stand out. First of all, a number of Lahoyans expressed a strong desire to learn about the city and city life. Second, in about half the interviews migrants phrased the motive for migration in terms of cultural and educational aspirations. These migrants saw the move as a way to continue studying, to learn to speak Spanish well, and to "defend" themselves better. Third, family conflicts were often cited in interviews as being the immediate motivation for deciding to leave the village. Typical among the responses given were those of marital conflict or the separation or death of one or both parents. In these cases it is quite possible that conflict in the family served as a kind of "last straw" that influenced people to make a final decision, but there may in fact have been other pressing factors that lay below the surface and that also supported the decision to leave (Arizpe 1975). A fourth and final factor was important during this period: factionalization and conflict within the village. This factor is treated in detail in the following chapter because it is related to the question of Lahoyan migrant associations in Mexico City.

As far as I could determine, the destination of migrants during the second stage of migration was almost exclusively Mexico City. The pull of the capital was so strong, in fact, that most of the migrants who went to Oaxaca City in the 1950s moved to the capital in the 1960s and 1970s. For the most part, it became clear to migrants that the number of jobs available, the wages, and (for those fortunate enough to obtain steady jobs in a modern industry) the working conditions and benefits were far superior to those available in Oaxaca City. As for the migrants leaving directly from the village, the growing number of Lahoyan families in Mexico City made it easy to find a relative or friend to sponsor the move or to facilitate adaptation. What follows are examples that illustrate what Lahoyan migrants said about the reasons behind their decision to migrate.

Beginning with an example of cultural or educational aspirations, Sr. Torre told me that his father was the crucial figure in his decision to leave Lahoya. Sr. Torre's father had insisted that his son get an education, and that was that. Sr. Torre was obliged to enroll in a boarding school for indigenous students located in the sierra. This was the first in a number of moves that eventually led him to the capital.

A closely related response, mentioned by many adults, both men and women, was that they left the village in order to learn to speak Spanish more fluently. Several women who came to Mexico City to work as maids mentioned their original interest in studying, but none of them were able to pursue this aspiration. As one of them pointed out, it is very difficult for Lahoyan women to combine work and education. At the very least, one must have guidance and aid in order to succeed. I am certain, though, that aspirational motives for migration are important to Lahoyans even if these are more modestly conceived and implemented compared to those of the Ralu'an migrants.

Another stated motive indicated that migrants were attracted to the image of the city. This was expressed by men and women who said that, back in the village, city life seemed so special. In fact, many Lahoyan migrants said that they came principally in order to see the city and to learn for themselves about city ways and city life. As one informant put it, he left Lahoya in 1959 and came directly to the capital, "para conocer el D.F." (to get to know the Federal District). This was the primary reason. His recollections of his life in those days was: "cambió todo" (everything changed); "me gustó" (I liked it); and, "para mi, era fantástico" (to me, it was fantastic).

In talking to people it became evident that migrants who return to Lahoya for visits are largely responsible for creating these images. Some people were extremely critical of this. One man emphasized that people from the village were "tricked" or "fooled" into going to the D.F. He explained that Lahoyans see their old friends return from the capital for a visit and that the latter are all dressed up and bring tales of their new job, new house, new life, and so forth, in the city, some of which are exaggerations if not outright lies. In effect, this man argued, some migrants convey the impression that it is a cinch to make one's way in the city. Only after living there for some time—and seeing the actual conditions, including discrimination—do the new migrants realize that there are significant disadvantages, too.

Finally, a number of cases in both periods can be grouped together in a residual category of motives—namely, "social" reasons for migration (Singer 1975:58). The first of these involves "passive migration," in which a person merely accompanies parents or relatives who have already made the decision to leave. This pertains mostly to children, who must perforce accompany their families, and to women who are sent to "keep house" for male relatives who are working and/or studying in Oaxaca or Mexico City. Another kind of social motive for leaving Lahoya has to do with marital or family conflicts. Migrants from Lahoya were surprisingly frank (from my point of view), stating that marital or family conflicts provoked their decision to leave the village, although usually this was not explained any further.

I also collected case histories of people who were orphans or whose parents had split up and were remarried. A number of individuals from Lahoya would explain, with a special emphasis, "I was an orphan," implying that this was a clear and understandable motive in itself. Further inquiry revealed that, locally, being an orphan meant that both or only one parent had died. In addition, while economic pressures often intensify with the death of a parent, many times the resulting pressure is interpersonal. An example of each follows.

A widow, Sra. José, said that her husband had died in an accident in the *campo* and that her children had been left orphans. There was no work for the two eldest daughters in Lahoya, so they decided to leave. They initially went down to Oaxaca City in 1958 without any idea of exactly what they were going to do to earn a living.

Señorita Martínez, on the other hand, said that, when her parents split up, she couldn't get along with the man her mother took up with. This was one of the reasons she felt impelled to leave the village. She did not want to get married, and there was no other escape from the difficulties she faced at home. In regard to such cases, Lahoyans commented that stepparents are just never the same as one's real parents.

OUT-MIGRATION FROM RALU'A

Although probably small numbers of persons have always left the town to go to other communities in the district, to the local mines at Natividad, or to Oaxaca City, significant out-migration to points of destination outside of the district began only after 1940.

Looking for a Life, 1940–1959

Beginning with the first period of substantive out-migration, from 1940 through 1959, two critical developments took place. For one, by the 1940s coffee had been established as the main cash crop grown in Ralu'a. Coffee production also became more general among farmers as a whole. Many grew some for their own consumption and sold small amounts of surplus production. Second, in these years roads and transportation slowly began to link the region with the Valley of Oaxaca and the nation. While contact had been steady since the colonial period, improved roads and transportation made such contact more frequent and regular.[2] This factor did not have a direct influence on agricultural methods, but it did promote the marketing and sale of cash crops, as well as increasing the levels of commerce. For Ralu'a, then, important changes involved the increasing production and marketing of coffee and the forging of a permanent link to the outside world through improved transportation, communication, and commerce. There was, however, no major change in agricultural technology during this period.

A number of "push" factors in the town had developed in the decade before this period. High birth rates, population increases, increasing pressure on land, and limited opportunities for day laborers all were present (Young 1978a). Wage labor was poorly remunerated, and interviews suggested that cycles of local depression were felt during this period, in part because of the long-term impact of the Mexican Revolution, which had closed mines and local industry in the sierra. Subsequently, the effects of the worldwide depression of the 1930s were also felt in the area. These were the two major developments that negatively affected the local economy and created increasing financial pressures on Ralu'ans.

Beginning in the 1940s, migration from Ralu'a to destinations outside the district began to increase. It is possible to identify a number of categories of persons who decided to leave the village during these years. One was stimulated by the bracero program, discussed in Chapter 3. Announcements of the program's temporary permits to work in the United States were issued in Oaxaca City and quickly reached back into the Sierra Juárez. As a result, the first two groups, totaling almost thirty men, left the town to work in various agricultural areas in the United States. Many of the braceros were from families who were doing well in Ralu'a but who wanted additional capital to finance commerce or the purchase of additional coffee lands (Nader, personal communication).

During this period a number of other youths left the town in order to continue their education. At this time Ralu'a was the only community in the area with a primary school. (Whatever their socioeconomic background, most of the populace received at least a primary-school education.) Since teachers are regarded with a good deal of respect, many Ralu'an families aspired to have one of their children attain the title of *professor*. Thus, a small number of families were able to gather enough money to send a son to study in the public school system in Oaxaca City. Perhaps because its educational system is more developed and because its Catholic orientation is strong, six or seven men and women also left the village to study in the seminary. In talking to informants it became clear that religious or secular education was seen as the only way to leave the village with some hope of a better future.

To recapitulate, some of the early migrants from Ralu'a belonged to a small elite group who saw out-migration as the pursuit of a vocation or the attainment of savings that could be used to improve their standard of living back home in the village. Another group of out-migrants was made up of young single men who left the area to become soldiers or to seek adventure and see the world. They were few in number. By 1950 the largest group of out-migrants consisted of young single men and women who went to Oaxaca City to look for work as servants and laborers. Their numbers are difficult to calculate, but I estimate that the total was between 75 and 100 and that more women than men left. Besides being young and single, these migrants were from families with little if any economic means.

According to the migrants I spoke to in Mexico City who migrated during this period, the most important factor that influenced them to leave Ralu'a was that work and wages were very limited then. These conditions affected families of limited socioeconomic means most directly. These families, although they might own a little land, fluctuated between taking care of small subsistence plots and selling wage labor to the wealthier villagers whenever there was work. The young, single members of these families left or were in effect sent away because within the town's economic system there was little hope of obtaining a measure of economic security, let alone a better standard of living. In short, the data indicate that the large majority of migrants who left during this period left for reasons tied to economic necessity.

In the cases I was able to collect, informants stressed either their personal economic duress or the general poverty and "backwardness" of Ralu'a in the 1950s.[3] In the former case, informants said the level of poverty was so extreme that they were literally left with no choice but to migrate if they wanted to better their situation. In the latter case, informants usually stressed that general poverty—produced by such factors as the lack of modern agricultural methods and the declining fertility of the soil—influenced them to leave. These kinds of responses also focused on the difficult and strenuous nature of agricultural labor. (This is a fact disputed by no one, actually, but it was nonetheless emphasized by only some of the migrants in their responses.) Running like a thread through these accounts was the fact that Ralu'ans recalled periods of intense suffering and difficulty when they talked about village life.

Other factors increased the possibility of considering out-migration as a reasonable alternative to village life. From the 1940s on, it became easier to leave, if only because of improvements in transportation. In addition, braceros and others returned to the village with stories of their travels and experiences. Because of the geographic isolation of the community, such reports served to instruct Ralu'ans generally about the conditions and possibilities in the city.

The Move to the Capital, 1960–1980

Three conditions that were already in existence in the previous period continued to intensify after 1960 and served to stimulate out-migration. These were the steady increase in the population (from both new births and in-migration from surrounding communities), increasing fragmentation of landholdings, and the lack of open land for expansion. All of these factors were exacerbated by the gradual reduction in the fertility of the soil (Eckholm 1977; Whitecotton 1977:319n5), challenges from neighboring communities that believed that Ralu'a had wrongfully obtained lands that could not legally be sold to private parties, and increasing demands for tequio labor. At the same time, no major economic changes took place during this period; crops, production techniques, tools, and other factors all appear to have remained the same.

In reviewing the historical data, there were two changes that, while not directly linked to modes of production, had important implications for the local economy. The first was the sharp drop in coffee prices in the mid-1950s (Young 1978a:140), which likely placed pressure on those who relied heavily on selling wage labor for their livelihood and on families who depended on selling coffee. Even the wealthiest families became aware of the dangers of Ralu'a's dependency on a single cash crop.[4] The second was the completion of a road into the village in 1959.

At the same time that these two structural changes were occurring, detailed information began to arrive in Ralu'a about urban occupations and urban life. Further, by then several of the Ralu'an migrants had been able to achieve relatively high levels of education and employment in Mexico City. As a result, more and more of the out-migrants went directly there. The growing number of paisanos in Mexico City, as well as wider fields of opportunity there, greatly influenced Ralu'ans' selection of the city as the preferred urban destination. Thus, when I first visited the town in 1975, even the Ralu'ans who had never visited the capital knew something about urban occupations and life in Mexico City.

In essence, the second major period of out-migration from Ralu'a involved a pattern of "chain migration." Chain migration occurs when early migrants arrive at an urban point of destination, see that superior occupational and educational opportunities are available there compared to opportunities in the point of origin, and begin to send for other family members, friends, and neighbors—in a word, paisanos—to join them. In this fashion, a special network is created that links the rural and urban spheres. Once such a network is created, it is both easy and convenient for migrants to move along this path. Chain migration, when accompanied by an explicit or implicit set of norms such as are entailed in the concept of paisanazgo, also effectively guarantees that new migrants have a set of hosts, friends, and potential facilitators waiting to help them once they arrive in the city (Price 1963; Alexander 1981; Goering 1989). When the sheer scale of opportunities in Mexico City became known in Ralu'a and the out-migrant community there reached some two hundred persons, a pattern of chain migration became firmly established. Other potential urban destinations were eliminated, and more and more Ralu'ans began to go directly to Mexico City.

The data indicate that patterns established earlier began to diversify during the second period of out-migration. For example, with respect to socioeconomic background, age, and educational level, a wider range of types of people began to leave Ralu'a. As before, migrants included single men and women between the ages of twenty and thirty. Increasingly, these single migrants paved the way; once established in the city, they would often send for other siblings and even their aged parents. In greater numbers than ever before, entire families began to migrate (or at least ended up in the city together after a short time). It is also notable that after 1960, while members of the poorer families continued to leave, for the first time members of the families of means also began to migrate in increasing numbers. That is to say that earlier migration began as a recourse for people who believed they had no future in the village, while in the 1960s, people left who did have a future in the village but who were looking for an even brighter future in the city.

I was able to interview many of these later migrants during my fieldwork in Mexico City. Whether I talked to young, single students or workers, to members of a nuclear family or an extended family, or to the rich or poor, people's motives for migration were characterized by a desire to progress and to improve their lives both culturally and occupationally. These were very strong and constant themes, notable because of the repetition of the Spanish terms *superarse* (to improve oneself) and *progresar* (to progress). In particular, the desire to find better work or a better salary, a better education for themselves or their children, or simply "to progress" in itself was constantly stressed.

Many of the migrants who came after 1960 repeatedly used catchwords like *aspiration, progress, development, and improvement* to explain why they had decided to go to Mexico City. When I asked Sr. Ramírez why he left, he said: "I left, just like the others leave Ralu'a, because I wanted to excel in life a little more." When I urged him to explain so that I could be sure to understand, he thought for a moment and then said:

> Well, most of the people who are leaving the provinces leave because they want to develop themselves, develop their lives. Each one of them looks to improve according to their background and possibilities. Some of them study, some of them work. There are many different reasons why people are leaving the provinces. As far as I can tell, it is a question of improvement. People are becoming more and more aware of what's going on.

In a related response, many people told me that they came to the city to obtain a better education. This desire applied both to parents who wanted to see their children study and to young adults who came specifically to study. Both saw education as a desirable means to obtain better jobs, better salaries, and a better life. The most fascinating example of the attraction of education and the prestige that it carried for Ralu'ans involved the children of wealthy families who defied parental wishes (and in some cases risked losing inheritances that would have guaranteed their security and livelihood) in order to go to the city and continue studying. One youth my own age even told me that, despite the fact that he had to disregard his father's wishes in order to go to Mexico City, he was not ungrateful, nor did he mean to be disrespectful. Rather, the idea of taking over the family store and running it for the rest of his life was unattractive to him because it represented no challenge: "I'd worked in the business already for years, and I knew I wanted something different."

Another aspect of the desire to progress involved the search for better work and a better salary. An older man, Sr. Jiménez, who had lived most of his life in the village, told me that he, his wife, and their three adult children had left the village together in 1969. "We came mainly so that our children could work. It's hard to earn and save a little money in Ralu'a, so we all decided together to come to the D.F. and give life here a try."

In short, when I asked Ralu'ans in Mexico City to explain their decision to migrate during the 1960s and 1970s, I found that, while many expressed dissatisfaction with the limitations of rural agricultural life in the sierra, this dissatisfaction was often overshadowed by the positive attraction of urban opportunities: better jobs, a better standard of living, a better education, and a chance for upward mobility.

Not everyone acknowledged the image of aspiration and achievement, however. One example that sticks in my mind involved a well-known and well-respected widower from Ralu'a who had been in the capital for some time. Sr. Pineda explained that competition is the dominant theme among the Ralu'ans in Mexico City, and a common goal is to be upwardly mobile. "Someone gets a degree," he said, "buys some new consumer goods, adds on to the house, purchases a new car, starts a new business. . . . Soon enough, all the paisanos find out about these new changes." Sr. Pineda claimed that such achievements on the part of others provoke envy and competition, and *that* is why Ralu'ans continually strive to develop and progress. "Nobody wants to be left behind, or for others to think that one is not as good as the rest," he emphasized.

There is one additional motive for migration among the Ralu'ans that does not fit into any of the above categories. By the late 1970s, some individuals and families had left Ralu'a for medical reasons. Medical care for serious illnesses is unavailable in Ralu'a, so if a serious illness develops and the people involved can afford it, the infirm and family members make a trip to Oaxaca City or Mexico City to seek medical advice and treatment. Sometimes, on this basis, people decide to move there permanently.

Finally, by the time I finished my fieldwork in 1979, migration from both Ralu'a and Lahoya had begun to level off, due to a number of factors. Besides the initiation of a government campaign against migration to the capital and the increasingly difficult urban conditions, rural wages for agricultural labor rose to unprecedented levels.[5]

OUT-MIGRATION FROM VILLA ALTA

Unfortunately, there is a paucity of data on the out-migration patterns of Villaltecos to Oaxaca or Mexico City. Suffice it to say that the outstanding characteristic of this case is the relatively high degree of pre-adaptation on the part of many out-migrants from the district seat. Traditionally an administrative, financial, and commercial center for the district, Villa Alta's position provided the basis for successful entrepreneurs like David Mendiolea to seek to establish businesses in Oaxaca City and beyond. Although Mendiolea apparently decided to move to and live in Oaxaca City, many successful merchants and officials prefer to remain in the sierra.

A second pattern evident before the 1960s is related to the fact that Villaltecos were among the first from the region to be able to obtain teaching credentials. Subsequently, some left the area to work in other parts of Oaxaca and other states, though a number returned to teach in district schools.

Since the town has also been the seat of government offices, including major branches of the national postal and telegraph offices, Villaltecos have long been able to familiarize themselves with these occupational specialties as well. This became an outstanding trend in the 1960s and 1970s, and many were able to pursue geographic and socioeconomic mobility as a result of exposure to and training in these occupations.

Beyond this, Mexican census data indicate that there were very heavy rates of out-migration from the district seat between 1960 and the 1980s. The urban points of destination of Villalteco out-migrants have probably been more diverse than those of Mountain Zapotecs from surrounding communities because of the availability of jobs in the areas of teaching and communications throughout the nation.

Summary

The initial group of migrants from Lahoya included both men and women. There was a small group of elite migrants composed of braceros and scholars, but this involved only twenty to thirty people. The majority of the migrants went to Oaxaca City to look for work as servants or in service-related occupations. Much like early migrants from the Rincón generally, these men and women were seeking a way to escape harsh conditions in their village of origin. They probably tended to come from families that owned little or no land.

A somewhat distinct group of migrants from Lahoya began to go directly to Mexico City in the 1960s. This group included migrants who had already lived for a time in Oaxaca City but increasingly also migrants who went directly from Lahoya to the capital. A large number of young women began to migrate from the village in order to look for jobs as maids. The village remained oriented toward self-provisioning, and there is no evidence to suggest that any new economic pressures impelled people to leave. Rather, the growing awareness of conditions and possibilities in the capital, including the growing number of paisanos, perhaps combined with increasing factionalism in the village, influenced landed peasants to seek new alternatives in the Federal District.

The data on Ralu'ans in Mexico City indicate that the people who left the town during the years from 1940 through 1959 tended to be single men and women who migrated in order to escape economic hardship. Most of these migrants belonged to the lower socioeconomic levels of the community. They were not from the poorest families but from families of small landholders who also worked as wage laborers. To the young men and women from these families, migration presented an alternative to a situation and problems that had no amelioration in the agricultural setting. In addition, small cohorts of emigrants left the town in order to pursue their education, to work as braceros, or to follow a spirit of adventure.

Another finding concerning the first period of out-migration from Ralu'a was that members of the wealthier families usually did not leave; they had everything they needed already. It is true that some of the entrepreneurs traveled regularly outside of the district, going to Oaxaca City or even Mexico City. Such trips were made to sell or purchase goods, however, and these men always returned to Ralu'a.

Another aspect of this first period was that Ralu'an out-migrants were drawn toward multiple points of destination. The most frequent of these was without doubt Oaxaca City, the nearest large city. The actual number is difficult to determine, but it appears that the total was between seventy-five and one hundred persons, largely women. Besides being young and single, these migrants tended to come from families of a low (but not the lowest) socioeconomic level.

The major drawback of Oaxaca City is that it was and remains a marketing center that offers only a limited number of jobs linked to modern industrial employment (Chance 1971:125; Murphy and Stepick 1991). Migrants from Ralu'a—men as well as women—tended to find employment in domestic work or service occupations. These were occupations such as being servants in houses or hotels, waiters in restaurants, or employees in bars, bathhouses, barbershops, or working in the street shining shoes or working as driver's assistants. All of these jobs were characterized by their low wages and lack of security and benefits. The same general occupational pattern is true of those individuals who migrated from Ralu'a to the various cities and towns of Veracruz and of the small number of families (perhaps twenty) that were scattered over other states of Mexico as far north as the border.

The bulk of Ralu'an migrants from 1960 on were still predominantly young, single men and women, but other kinds of individuals and domestic groups also began to leave the town. While these migrants sometimes mentioned dissatisfaction with the limitations of rural agricultural life as their motive for leaving, rather than dwelling on these limitations they were more likely to stress the opportunities available in Mexico City. The capital of the nation was the point of destination to such an extent that even those back in the Rincón who had never visited Mexico City could discuss general conditions and possibilities for upward mobility there. Passive migration takes place among the Ralu'ans in the same fashion as among the Lahoyans, although it probably occurs even more frequently among the Ralu'ans.

In contrast to the cases of Ralu'a and Lahoya, out-migrants from Villa Alta have generally been better prepared, both linguistically and occupationally, whether they left before or after 1960. As in the other two cases, there was some out-migration from Villa Alta during the 1940s and 1950s, but Villaltecos left in increasing numbers between 1960 and 1980. Clearly, because the Villaltecos speak Spanish and live in the district seat, they have been better able to pursue employment in professional fields like teaching and in national communications.

Finally, it is important to keep in mind that the long-term impact of out-migration has affected each community differently. For example, from 1940 through 1975 the population of Ralu'a grew to 2,000 despite the fact that the village lost about a quarter of its native-born population. By 1981 the village had a population of well over 2,000 (Nader, personal communication). The stability of the population figure in spite of extensive out-migration is explained by the fact that in-migrants have been continuously attracted to Ralu'a from the surrounding villages by the availability of work there. The population of Lahoya, by comparison, has dropped quite markedly since its peak of 934 in 1950. By 1980 there were only 416 inhabitants, and many of the young people had left. This large drop in population became one more link in a chain of increasing stagnation, since the lack of male citizens began to curtail the amount of work that the municipal government could demand.

In Villa Alta, many youths have chosen to migrate to Oaxaca and Mexico City, and they have often pulled family members to the capital once they have become settled. Birth rates and rates of in-migration from villages in the hinterland have not been enough to keep the population level stable. Through the 1970s and 1980s, Villa Alta experienced a sharp population decline similar in proportion to that of Lahoya. Nonetheless, although the political power of the district seat has been subject to challenge (Parnell 1988), Villa Alta remains the administrative center of the district.

MOTIVES FOR OUT-MIGRATION

At this point I would like to offer an analysis of the motives for out-migration that I identified among the two groups of Rincón Zapotec migrants I studied. This analysis is based on the assumption that human action has meaning for its participants; that is, statements on motives for migrating reveal, to some extent, the explicit and articulated meanings of migration from Zapotec points of view.

In the case of the migrants from Ralu'a, I found that the largest proportion of responses were those given by the recent migrants, who stressed the occupational and educational opportunities in the city. In smaller proportions, Ralu'an migrants would speak of grinding poverty that forced them to leave, or marital or family conflicts that drove them from the town. Strictly economic motives for migration were usually given by the early migrants.

By comparison, it is very evident from any extensive interview or life history that poverty is a very prominent aspect of everyday life in Lahoya. As

Table 5.1
Motives for Out-Migration by Theme and Orientation

	Push	Pull
Economic	poverty in the village	urban jobs
Social	family/factional conflict in the village	facilitation through kin/network ties
Aspirational	no opportunity in the village	more opportunity in the city

a motive for migration, however, poverty was only mentioned on occasion and was emphasized by only a small group of the earlier migrants. The later and more numerous group often cited family and factional conflicts. Many also articulated aspirational motives to explain why they came to the capital. Compared to Ralu'ans, their aspirations were more modest: to continue and finish primary school and, if possible, to get a higher education; to learn to speak Spanish well; and to learn about city life and city ways.

How can we best interpret this information? One possibility is to construct a framework that identifies some of the primary features of stated motives of migration. Three of these can be derived from the content of the statements themselves, that is, their economic, social, and aspirational content. Another dimension to these motives is found in the expression given to the content; the motive is phrased either in terms of a push factor that the migrant experienced in the point of origin or a pull factor that is perceived as existing in the point of destination. These features can be used to construct the six-celled framework shown in Table 5.1.

The immediate advantage of this framework is that it helps to clarify and simplify emic statements about migration and relate them to historical periods and structural conditions. For example, it is easier now to point out that, during the early periods of migration, Ralu'an and Lahoyan migrants emphasized the push factors in migration when they talked about their experiences and perceptions, and that they left because of precarious socioeconomic situations.[6]

The Ralu'an migrants who came after 1960 and who were able to take advantage of a full range of mutual aid via the larger migrant community, perceived and emphasized the pull factors in migration to the city. The migrants from Ralu'a who highlighted the opportunities available in the city also came from the middle socioeconomic strata of the town (that is, those with some land and resources) and generally arrived after 1960. Large numbers of these migrants came to the capital because they were discouraged by the constraints of a limited land base and the precariousness of cash cropping, but they migrated only after they felt assured of relative success in the city. From their point of view, progress and development had always been part of their experience in and view of Ralu'a, and they were continuing to pursue this tradition by going to and living in the capital. Thus it is possible to see how each period generated its own conditions and that these conditions were often reflected in the statements of informants as they talked about their lives and perceptions with respect to migration. Next I would like to address some of the variations that came up in interviews that do not fit into the above framework.

To begin with, in some cases motives are reversed, with early migrants from Ralu'a stressing aspirational motives and later migrants emphasizing poor economic conditions in the village. In the former situation, the informants usually belong to one of the elite groups of early migrants: braceros, priests, and scholars. Because of their vocations (and sometimes their connections) they were able to pursue opportunities that were not ordinarily available. In the latter case, migrants usually came from lower socioeconomic levels within the community of origin and lacked ties to out-migrants in the city before they left.

Another question about the variation of motives is, Why do so many of the Lahoyan migrants emphasize the aspirational (pull) aspects of migration? At first glance this seems strange, especially since Lahoya is a relatively isolated village that has stagnated economically. But the key to the responses of these migrants lies in the stigmatization that Lahoyans have suffered in the sierra. Life in Lahoya revolves around farming and thus is associated with the difficulty of constant physical labor and a subsistence-level standard of living. Perhaps the economic hardships of life in the village are not emphasized precisely because the villagers know them so well, and they are indeed obvious to anyone who has been to the sierra. Yet, in my opinion, the Lahoyan migrants have come to accept the judgment of the surrounding communities that Lahoya is one of the poorest and seemingly most traditional of the Mountain Zapotec communities in the area. By migrating out of this situation, Lahoyans hoped to complete an education, gain command of the Spanish language, make a good living, and attain the lifestyle of the capital and the nation. It is at once a step for Lahoyans into the life of contemporary, modern Mexico and a means to gain more control over their own lives and destinies.

One final question about variation in motives is, Why is family conflict mentioned so often as the "last straw" that influenced potential migrants actually to leave? Clearly, the family (and usually the nuclear family) is the primary unit of production and consumption in the communities of the Sierra Juárez. Concomitantly, since the coordination of activities in a household is especially important in agricultural work, there are established norms of interaction and authority. In a town like Ralu'a, where the father is regarded as the absolute head of the family, intrafamilial relations tend to be hierarchical and authoritarian. Wives, unmarried women, and youths are often the most subject to traditional constraints and sanctions within the family setting. Not surprisingly, it is these people who perceive out-migration as one of the few ways to escape from a bad family situation. This is not to say that stress and strain were not present in Mountain Zapotec families in the area prior to 1940. While stress and strain surely did exist before, custom and tradition were stronger, and travel out of the sierra was arduous. Only in the last thirty years has out-migration become a real alternative to the pressures of domestic life in the village.

In concluding this section I would like to emphasize that in focusing on the stated motives for migration I do not mean to imply that, by themselves, they explain or fully account for the final decision to leave the sierra, or that they can be considered independently of economic and other contexts. However, the stated motives for migration expressed by Mountain Zapotec migrants *do* reflect a cultural order of meaning and perception. For this reason I have taken the stated motives for migration at their face value and have tried, first, to categorize them in terms of their common thematic content and then to show how the common motives for migration have their basis in, and often reflect, (1) the period during which migration took place, (2) the socioeconomic backgrounds of the migrants, and (3) the conditions in the urban point of destination (which have been briefly mentioned and which are discussed at greater length in the following chapter).

CONCLUSION

What conditions in the Sierra Juárez have made migration from this area different from that from, say, the central highlands of Mexico? To begin with, the Sierra Juárez and the central highlands are marked by distinct forms of economic and political organization. The agricultural system of production in the sierra has not been based on either large *latifundias* or *haciendas*. Rather, landholdings are small, typically under five hectares. The limited possibility of using either irrigation or modern machinery on the steep mountains of the sierra has effectively limited the size and productivity of landholdings. Thus the situation in the sierra has not been like that of the central highlands, in which indigenous populations have been systematically dominated by mestizo landowners, businessmen, and politicians who, in alliance, control the region's land, credit, and resources and who have profited from the entrance of agribusiness (Stavenhagen 1976). We must also recognize that the sierra is much more distant from the capital than are the central highlands and was much more geographically isolated before 1980 because of its relatively poor system of transportation. By comparison, migration from the central highlands to Mexico City was much easier, and out-migrants were able to move back and forth between their homes and the capital to a far greater extent than out-migrants from the sierra. In short, variations in migration patterns reflect the differing socioeconomic and ethnic composition of the two points of origin.

Specifically, my research indicates that there have been two broad patterns of migration from the Villa Alta district. One is represented by the Lahoyan case: migrants are typically young, single men and women who are forced out of the rural area by an increasingly circumscribed economy there (especially for families without means), as well as changing expectations about lifestyles and standards of living. Another marked feature of this pattern is that large numbers of women leave to look for work as maids in cities (see Young 1978a, 1978b, 1982). This broad pattern characterized out-migration from the district as a whole during the 1940s and 1950s, and from the poorer agricultural villages in the hinterlands throughout the period under consideration.

At the same time, there was a second broad pattern of out-migration from regional centers such as Ralu'a and Villa Alta that predominated after 1960 and that occurred when peasants from the middle and upper strata in the relatively more developed communities decided to leave to attain socioeconomic mobility. To some extent, out-migration continued to reflect the difficulties of agricultural life in the sierra, but more important was the fact that the unique opportunities available in settings like Mexico City seemed more accessible due to mutual aid available to new migrants after 1960. These conditions correlate with the stated motives of post-1960 migrants from the regional centers, which emphasized education, progress, and personal development.

CHAPTER 6

The Regional Bases of Migrant Social Relations

Although kinship was frequently a basis for facilitation, paisanazgo was the rationale I repeatedly heard migrants articulate to explain their intentions as well as their actions. This chapter describes both informal uses of paisanazgo—usually occurring between individuals or between individuals and families—and formal uses, characterized by the formation of migrant associations at the village, regional, or district level. The chapter highlights the situation that evolved between 1960 and 1980 in Mexico City, although it also includes material about Lahoyans and Ralu'ans in Oaxaca City between the 1940s and 1960.

LAHOYAN MIGRANTS

Facilitation and mutual aid were extensively practiced among members of the Lahoyan migrant community in Oaxaca City, which was the first primary urban point of destination after World War II. Lahoyans recalled that the street called Armenta López in Oaxaca City was famed among paisanos for its large settlement of Lahoyan migrants. In the later 1950s it was possible to arrive in Oaxaca City and get lodgings there even if one arrived without advance notice—though it might be only the corner of a room on a *petate*, or mat.

Lahoyans pursued three kinds of jobs in Oaxaca City. The first entailed work in bakeries. Many were brought into the trade by just one Lahoyan migrant who would first recommend paisanos as day laborers. If they enjoyed making sweet breads and cookies and were willing to work hard, he tried to help them obtain stable employment in the business.

A second occupational concentration involved work as waiters in the hotels around the central plaza. Three Lahoyans in particular were well known as having obtained work for many of their paisanos. Even though employed in some of the fanciest hotels in Oaxaca City, like the Marqués del Valle, there was not much future in this line of work, economically or professionally, so many of these men eventually migrated to Mexico City during the 1960s.

The third area of occupational concentration was in domestic service. Both men and women did such work, although women predominated. Because of gender roles, and because I was a young, single foreigner, I had little access to Lahoyan women, but in the course of visiting a Lahoyan family in Mexico City, one man's wife was willing to share her experiences with me. Sra. Reyes told me that her father had brought her to Oaxaca City as a young girl. He went into a store to buy a shawl and actually persuaded the owner (a woman) to employ his daughter as a maid and even for the woman to become the girl's godmother. Sra. Reyes said that she acquiesced in the arrangement because her father wanted her to learn Spanish and she herself wanted to learn about Oaxaca City.

Some time later, while Sra. Reyes was standing in a doorway in Oaxaca City, a woman came along out of the blue and asked her if she wanted to go to Mexico City. She said yes since she wanted to get to know the capital, and the United States, too, if possible. The woman took her to the capital and put her to work in her home, located in a middle-class neighborhood. She said that, unfortunately, her new employer turned out to be very cruel. Sra. Reyes, who was only fourteen years old at the time, was locked in the house and made to work like a slave. Her employer would even hit and kick her. It was only after a long period of suffering, she told me, that one of the paisanos who had been in the capital for many years was able to remove her from this unfortunate situation. Sra. Reyes's woman's story is significant because, if there was one salient theme running through all of the interviews pertaining to this early period of out-migration, it was the prejudice and discrimination that the Lahoyans encountered in Oaxaca City.

When I met one of the early migrants who seemed relatively open to talking about such experiences, I asked in detail about how early migrants were treated. Sr. Domínguez explained that during the 1940s and 1950s the average migrant from Lahoya did not know how to speak Spanish very well, let alone read, and Oaxaqueños often made fun of such "deficiencies." Based on his own experiences, Sr. Domínguez emphasized that people would frequently repeat mistakes in grammar, malapropisms, and other errors right back in his face, imitating his bad accent as well. Another cruel practice was to make a mistake or a mispronunciation into a nickname that stuck forever to the "offender."

Similar experiences occurred on the job. Sr. Domínguez explained that in Lahoya one became familiar with basic farming tools at best—the hoe, the machete, the shovel, and the pick. In the city, by contrast, one was unfamiliar with the tools, their names, their uses, and actually with urban wage labor itself. Sr. Domínguez remembered that these shortcomings and ignorance were seized upon by the more fortunate as evidence of limited capacity and even inferiority. He remembered terms like *estúpido, pinche indio,* and other degrading insults being used daily. Interestingly enough, Sr. Domínguez also went on to say that many Mexicans just did not realize that "bad government" was the cause of all this; that *serranos,* or people of the sierra, were the way they were because the government had not given them a chance to obtain an education or the opportunity to advance.

In the course of interviews like this one, I often wondered if the memories I evoked troubled the Mountain Zapotec I talked to. So many of the stories of their early experiences involved hardship and suffering. With Sr. Domínguez, I sensed that, while he had had some difficult experiences, he had been able to sort things out and conclude that, although he had been insulted and even persecuted at times, there was nothing wrong with him personally or culturally.

In short, in interview after interview, migrants indicated that Spanish, as a second language, caused tremendous anxiety for many Zapotec peasants who ventured into the city during the 1940s and 1950s. Poor Spanish language skills elicited verbal abuse and other forms of prejudicial treatment remembered with a great deal of pain by migrants from Lahoya (as well as many of the early migrants from Ralu'a, I might add). After 1950, the larger towns in the sierra began to manifest ever-increasing links with the outside world, and ever since, Spanish-language proficiency has increased in the area. Villagers in the remote hinterlands, however, continued to be predominantly monolingual, even though children studied Spanish in school.

Mexico City

Compared to Oaxaca City, very few migrants from Lahoya went to Mexico City in the early 1950s. Facilitation in the capital was impossible due to the low numbers of migrants and the fact that most of those who were there were not in a financial position to help others. As in Oaxaca, women in the Federal District tended to be employed in domestic service, while men worked as servants, found jobs in the service sector, or sold wage labor in unskilled manual jobs in the informal sector of the urban economy.

By the late 1950s, the number of Lahoyan migrants in Mexico City had grown substantially. It had become evident to Lahoyans in Oaxaca City, as well as in the village, that the capital offered the widest range of occupational and educational opportunities. At this point, the increased possibility of receiving help from relatives or paisanos influenced many people to make the move to the capital. The range of types of migrants broadened.

In one example of how paisanazgo figured into occupational facilitation, a Lahoyan migrant, Sr. Salazar, got a job at a company that produced furniture. He was a reliable employee, so management accepted his recommendations about hiring fellow Lahoyans, and these men in turn recommended other paisanos. Apparently there were as many as fifty men from Lahoya working in this factory at one time. In the end, though, the furniture company let all of them go because the management did not want to employ any individual for too long a time—by law, worker compensation payments were made according to the length of time a worker has been employed.

A second example involves a sociable, genial gentleman I will call Don Fernández. Don Fernández had a job at Mexico City's Spanish Club, where he came to know many of the clients. He eventually made friends with some Spaniards who ran a furniture factory and was able to recommend that they hire some of his paisanos from Lahoya who were looking for jobs. Not long after, Don Fernández also recommended paisanos to a Spaniard who was running a very successful chain of bakeries. These men did very well, and they in turn recommended others. Although their pay was low, especially in the beginning, this turned out to be a great boon for the Lahoyans in the capital, since the chain employed a great many workers and the individual shops were scattered around the city. Don Fernández, as the Lahoyans referred to him, continued to work at the club and never himself worked at the furniture factory or as an employee of the bakery.

Similarly, Sr. González said his employers often appreciated the sincere, dedicated attitude of the Lahoyan workers, and because of this he had been fairly successful at recommending his paisanos for jobs: "They are punctual, they try not to miss a day, they really work hard, and they are honest." Sr. González noted that this was why his bosses often forgave an individual when, as sometimes occurred, a migrant dropped everything and vanished, needing to go to back to Lahoya on some pressing business.

Sr. González said that work in the capital was very different from work out in the fields. For one thing, in Lahoya most families obtain cash income by selling surplus crops or produce; thus, they have a little money only once or twice a year. By contrast, in Mexico City workers receive a weekly salary. Sr. González noted that this was why Lahoyans, after they had saved a bit of money, especially liked to purchase nice clothes, eat well, and buy items to make their domestic life more convenient and enjoyable. Thus, once Lahoyan migrants obtained a job they liked and that paid fair wages, they were usually quite dedicated to their work. They appreciated a job that offered a steady salary and thus security, as well as access to consumer goods.

As these cases indicate, mutual aid between kin and paisanos has been very valuable to Lahoyan migrants in terms of occupational opportunity. At the same time, migrants acknowledged that overall facilitation was necessarily limited in its duration. Few families could promise indefinite lodging, meals, or support, even for close relatives. Still, the migrant community could provide moral support that could be critical in times of difficulty or need.

I learned, for example, that some of the maids were single mothers with small children. In one case, the father had refused to marry a Lahoyan woman. She came from a large family, and her male cousins in Mexico City (all of whom were about her own age) visited regularly and did their best to be "uncles" for the child. This was not an uncommon situation, either among the Lahoyans or among the poorer women who left Ralu'a. From time to time, both Lahoyan and Ralu'an men would comment darkly that the young women who came to work in the capital as maids were naive, so they suffered greatly. Although I could not obtain any figures, I was told that maids were sometimes taken advantage of. Apparently the men who do this were not necessarily their employers but rather boyfriends from the capital or sometimes even serranos, who got them pregnant and then left them to fend for themselves.

Between 1960 to 1970, during a period of economic growth in Mexico City, Lahoyan migrants obtained new experience and skills, and patterns of occupation and mobility changed. Despite a continuing prevalence of domestic work for women and wage labor for men, by the middle of the 1970s many men held "tenured" jobs (i.e., jobs protected by formal contract) that paid steady minimum wages. At the same time, occupational histories indicate that Lahoyans' work experiences were still characterized by stigmatization, frequent horizontal mobility, shifts in and out of formal-sector occupations, and periods of unemployment. Since the educational attainment of the Lahoyan migrants was low (through no fault of their own), they were the first to suffer from the standard policy among many Mexican companies in the 1970s of firing unskilled and semiskilled workers before they could obtain tenure or before their "compensatory" payments became too high.

Young unmarried women continued to migrate to Mexico City throughout the 1970s specifically to work as maids. Many "lived in," although some chose to work by day, and most were employed in middle-class neighborhoods like Roma, Del Valle, and Polanco. Like Señorita Martínez, women were attracted by the image of good, steady wages and comparatively favorable working conditions.

Sra. Rodríguez, however, said that she originally left the village with the hope of studying but that this proved impossible. She said that her brother, who was already living in the capital, brought her directly to Mexico City and found her employment in a matter of days as a nurse, caring for young children. She was "kept inside" for three months and had to learn Spanish "out of necessity." Sra. Rodríguez remembered that she accomplished this with much effort and that in the beginning she had to use hand signs to communicate with her employers. When I inquired if she had ever felt slighted, she said that in all honesty, since she was completely unable to understand Spanish in the beginning, her employers may have actually been insulting her or swearing at her the whole time. We laughed, and then she reiterated that she did not really know. Sra. Rodríguez said that, all in all, even though the period of initial adjustment was difficult, she enjoyed Mexico City. She began to go out after a while—to the street or out to the market. Over the years, her Spanish gradually improved and she felt that she was finally "learning new things." By 1979 this pattern of migration and domestic work for young women appeared to be slackening but had not stopped entirely.

In the late 1970s, according to best estimates, the population of Lahoyan migrants in Mexico City was about three hundred adults, making them one of the three largest Rincón Zapotec migrant communities in the capital. Data on Lahoyan households in the 1970s were limited but indicated that most arrangements involved either nuclear families or nuclear families extended by the inclusion of close relatives. The latter were often being facilitated until they were able to move out on their own.

One way to account for the extension of urban families is Sr. González's explanation that Lahoyans feel that, when paisanos are new, it is necessary to give them a place to live and food to eat. Aid is given to new migrants because earlier migrants can remember all too well what it was like to be alone and to suffer in the city. Established migrants thus do their best to see that others will not have to go through the suffering they endured. This obligation is so strong that often a new migrant can go to kin or paisanos in Mexico City and simply expect them to help out. Migrants from Lahoya who have lived in Mexico City for some time, however, are expected to look out for themselves as best they can. At any rate, if offering aid is not possible, or if there is any suspicion about the sincerity or need of the recipient, an excuse or a refusal is considered appropriate.

Outside of initial lodging, orientation, and help with finding a job, the majority of case studies I gathered concerning mutual aid among Lahoyans involved events and situations having to do with migrants' "difficulties" in the capital. Many of the difficulties were rooted in the language barrier. I learned that a number of people, especially young men and women working as servants in private homes, had to be rescued from "difficult" situations. Several of these men and women were even jailed because they were not able to express or defend themselves adequately in Spanish. In more than one case, injustices occurred over what turned out to be misunderstandings or misperceptions. Fortunately, long-term migrants were sometimes able to come to the rescue of the falsely imprisoned.

Many of the Lahoyan migrants have land and houses in the capital and have settled in neighborhoods in proximity to compatriots from the village. Three of these areas are on the periphery of Mexico City, and two were founded by invading the land; that is, small groups of Lahoyan migrants claimed land by participating in popular (i.e., non-Zapotec) squatter movements. Because of residential clustering, patterns of interaction and reciprocity between Lahoyans in such neighborhoods can have a strong day-to-day basis, especially when they are reinforced by kinship or work relationships.

Although it is somewhat exceptional, an outstanding example of a network formed on this basis is the Grupo Progreso, a kind of neighborhood-based migrant association organized by Lahoyans from the Progreso district (*colonia*) on the southern periphery of Mexico City. While informal in nature, the Grupo Progreso has provided a number of services for its members, including helping Lahoyan members to cover funeral expenses. By the end of the 1970s, this group was also becoming directly involved in issues of home-village development. This was, incidentally, the only group among the Mountain Zapotec I know of in which women have played a formal leadership role.

Initially, migrant social organization took the form of informal social networks. As mentioned above, these networks were based on ties of paisanazgo and encompassed a diverse mix of relationships, including kinship, neighborhood status, a common workplace or occupation, and mutual interests. Parties and leisure activities like sports were the main events that brought Lahoyan migrants together. In the late 1950s, for example, young women who had come to Mexico City to work as maids used to gather every weekend for a party and invited their friends. Everyone who attended contributed money to help pay for food and a crate of soft drinks.

Two other networks began to cluster at the homes of two early migrants, both of whom had prestige among their compatriots because they had achieved professional careers. One of the latter networks was centered around parties at the house of a man who had been born in Lahoya but who had grown up in Mexico City. This man (whom I will refer to as the professor) had been orphaned at an early age. Brought to the capital as a child, he was eventually able to complete his education at an institute that trained elementary-school teachers. The professor was thus well educated by village standards. This, along with the fact that his accomplishments were achieved despite difficult personal circumstances, was greatly admired by his paisanos. Over the years, he had also established many political connections throughout the official bureaucracies in Mexico City and Oaxaca City, which he was eventually able to put to good use on behalf of his fellow villagers.

The more formal dimension of the social organization of the Lahoyan migrants in Mexico City, which revolved around two migrant village associations, has evolved through distinct stages and so must be seen from an historical point of view.

Lahoyan Village Associations

In the course of many gatherings at his house during the late 1950s, the professor came up with several ideas, all of which revolved around projects to improve the basic infrastructure of Lahoya. Such projects had the potential for being funded by the Mexican government, especially since the national policy at that time was to extend basic services into the rural hinterlands.

Finding that there was great enthusiasm among his compatriots regarding these ideas, the professor eventually decided to organize a formal village association in Mexico City, named the Lahoyan Development Association, to carry out these projects. Although the association had no formal (that is, written) charter, it did have a set of offices (*patronatos*). Candidates could run for office, and officers were popularly elected by the members of the association. Terms were apparently more or less permanent, lasting until a candidate stepped down from office.

Having heard of the professor's plans, the leader of the second main network of migrants—also a formal village association by then—agreed to work with the professor for the common benefit of Lahoya. The two leaders thus decided to merge their groups and take turns being the president of a single unified migrant association. The professor took the first turn and quickly took control of the organization. He was able to do this largely because of his ability to draw on his many personal contacts and friends in the middle echelons of the federal government. Through these contacts the professor was able to petition for and obtain the funding and technical assistance to initiate a series of village development projects.

As an example of how this process worked, the village's telephone service (a single line that linked Lahoya to the telegraph office in Ralu'a) was rapidly initiated and completed between 1958 and 1959. Under the administration of Mexican president Ruiz Cortines, the federal government had set up a special program to provide such telephone service to remote areas, so funds and technical support were definitely available. The professor knew of this program and through his connections was able to get federal and state funding.

For their part, the citizens of Lahoya participated in tequios in order to clear selected areas for the posts that were to be installed for the line. Neighboring villages were invited to send work teams to help, but they apparently declined to participate because they believed that the telephone service would not be of any direct benefit to them.

When the telephone line was completed, there was a formal inauguration on July 5, 1959. Officials from the Department of Communications came up to the village from Oaxaca and Mexico City in honor of the accomplishment. Shortly afterward, however, a man from a prominent family in Lahoya wrote a letter to officials charging that improprieties were taking place in the use of the system. The professor's followers were quick to discover this accusation and sent representatives back to the village to challenge these allegations informally through the medium of public opinion.

The plan for the electrification of Lahoya was another of the professor's ideas. With the completion of the telephone line, he made electrification a full-scale project. Again, under the administration of Ruiz Cortines, federal government funding and technical support were being extended to rural areas specifically to encourage such installations.

The *palanca* (or lever) in this case (according to one source), was a deputy who was able to get the professor an appointment with Ruiz Cortines. This gained the project initial attention. Subsequently, engineers came to assess the situation as early as 1959, although nothing immediately came of this visit. Later on, in 1968, the government sent a representative from the Lighting Commission (Comisión de Luz), who checked things out and also left without making any promises. Nothing else transpired until around 1973. Everything seemed to have been forgotten when suddenly, out of the blue, engineers from the Lighting Commission arrived and began putting up posts. While the Lahoyan villagers had always assumed that electric wires would follow the road and had engaged in tequio labor to prepare for the installation with this idea in mind, the wires were actually strung in a line from Ralu'a through the intervening villages and straight on to Lahoya. In some cases, observers commented, engineers simply placed two posts on either side of a huge valley and strung the wire between them.

Work toward the construction of a passable road—without doubt the most important of the projects conceived and initiated by the professor—also began in 1959. The professor began to make petitions (*gestiones*) that year, again to sympathetic agencies and officials who were under government orders to encourage and support rural development projects. At the time the petitions were being considered, work on a road into Lahoya had already been started. Initial efforts used tequio labor exclusively and were perhaps inspired by the completion of a passable road into Ralu'a.

Although the village realized definite achievements during this period, overt factionalism within the unified Lahoyan migrant village association also began to occur as early as 1959. The nature of the division is not fully clear, but it appears that the professor was unwilling to yield the leadership position once his term of office was technically over. Since only the professor had government contacts and since payments for projects were issued in his name, it was almost impossible for any opponent or rival leader to unseat him.[1]

Believing that the initial promise to share the leadership position had been broken, the leader of the other group of Lahoyan migrants became angry and withdrew, taking all of his people with him. This split, which occurred in about 1960, was definitive and final. Subsequently, the two leaders and their respective followers were at odds for many years. In addition, because the members of elite families in Lahoya had their own contacts at the local and state levels of government, they had been able to launch their own program to undermine the professor and his group. With the split between the two groups in 1960, the rival leader in Mexico City, who was opposed to the professor, threw his support to the leading families back in Lahoya. Thus the division of the migrant community in Mexico City was soon replicated in corresponding divisions in Lahoya itself as well as in Oaxaca City. In the following decade, animosity and conflict became quite intense between the professor's association, the rival association in Mexico City, affiliated groups in Oaxaca City, and factions within Lahoya itself.

Through his many connections in the government bureaucracy (and with a great deal of time and work), the professor was eventually able to obtain partial funding for the road from the Department of Local Roads (Departamento de Caminos Vecinales). Under the terms of the agreement, resources were supposed to come from federal funds and two other sources—the state of Oaxaca, and the village itself. In the end, the state never gave any of the promised money and, due to financial considerations more than anything else, village contributions were limited to tequio labor.

Federal financing began in 1960 and lasted through 1968. Payments were made for the completion of specific segments of the road, so work took place installment by installment. During this period, because of the government grant, Lahoyan villagers were compensated for the time and labor they spent on construction work. This was a token amount, however, in the sense that the salaries were not large enough for anyone to give up farming and support himself in this manner. When I inquired about it, a good part of the monies were said to have gone to pay the salary of an engineer whose job was to plan and supervise the overall implementation of the project.

Because the professor was studying to be a lawyer but had already missed taking the bar exams for two years running because he was spending so much time and effort on this project, he decided to stop petitioning for money in 1968. At this point, three-fourths of the new road had been completed, and the fourth that remained had already been mapped out by the engineer. The plan for the last fourth of the road called for a completely new route into Lahoya, avoiding the paths that had been used for decades. For this reason, it was called the *traza técnica* (the technically sound route) by the professor's supporters.

Despite the positive achievements, factionalism continued over the years. To cite one example, in 1968 a man of some influence in Lahoya learned that the professor had gone to Oaxaca City to pick up a check for a section of roadwork. The man was able to stir up the pueblo by suggesting that the professor was pocketing this money and that it was not really being used for the road at all. The village municipal government actually issued a formal charge along these lines, but when the police went to detain the professor, all of the pertinent papers and permits were found to be in order, so the charges were dropped.

Interestingly enough, the Lahoyans became concerned at this point that intracommunity factionalism might impede efforts to obtain further government support for development projects. On September 28, 1968, a number of community leaders got together to pledge cooperation and to commit the moral and financial resources of the village as a whole to the progress and benefit of Lahoya. They even went so far as to draw up and sign a formal document to this effect. Nonetheless, because conflicts continued to arise, it became clear that intracommunity divisions were not going to be overcome very easily. Moreover, by this time each group had its own set of ties to external agencies: the leading families of Lahoya tended to appeal to officials in the district seat of Villa Alta, while the professor's group had ties to state officials in Oaxaca City.

In the heat of many struggles—struggles that resulted in old friendships being torn asunder and even death threats being issued that were designed to silence the principal actors—some of the Lahoyans in Mexico City began to drop out of the migrant community in hopes of avoiding further struggles and controversies.

Suddenly and unexpectedly, in 1970 the professor was killed under mysterious circumstances. Some claimed he had been hit by a car outside of a house where he had attended a party that evening; others said his body bore marks of an assault that the supposed "hit and run" was designed to cover. No one was ever apprehended or charged in regard to his death. Soon afterward, the leadership of the rival association, in alliance with elite families in Lahoya, felt that they now had an opportunity to get everyone together again under their newly asserted guidance and leadership. This vision, however, turned out to be quite difficult to realize. The professor, it should be noted, almost never took his paisanos to meetings with government officials. He kept his contacts to himself and, it should be remembered, arranged to receive all project payments directly. Consequently, when he died, all of the funding links were broken. Federal aid was never again obtained at the same level for any Lahoyan development project, including the completion of the road.

After his untimely death, one key point of contention had to do with monies that the professor had obtained and placed in the bank to pay for completing the road. After failing to receive a satisfactory response when they called upon the members of the professor's association to relinquish the funds that had been deposited in reserve, the head of the rival association—again in conjunction with members of prominent Lahoyan families—invited a number of government officials to attend a special meeting of Lahoyans called in Oaxaca City in late 1970.

At this meeting, the leadership of the late professor's association still refused to comply with demands to surrender the money. The opposition then presented charges of corruption and fraud against the professor's group to Oaxacan officials, charges that made front-page headlines in Oaxaca City newspapers. Because substantial progress had actually been made on the road, when the case was brought to court there was simply not enough evidence to support the charges, and the case was dismissed. Nevertheless, the battle had reinforced the division between the different Lahoyan factions.

With a quarter of the new road still to be constructed, the professor's opponents decided to complete the project, but in their own fashion. First, Lahoyan villagers were expected to do the rest of the job on the basis of unpaid tequio labor alone; the village municipio agreed only to provide food for the laborers. Second, perhaps because they wanted to assert that the completion of the road was due to their own initiative and efforts, the opposition decided to ignore the route proposed by the engineer (the traza técnica). Instead, they decided to complete the final fourth of the road by widening an old path that had traditionally linked Lahoya and Ralu'a. Unfortunately, this path was located on a very steep incline. Thus, when the job was finished in 1971, the road was quite poor. It was difficult, for example, for a loaded truck to traverse the road even during the dry season; during the rainy season the road was basically impassable. In short, after years of great sacrifice and labor there was little to show for all the effort.

Back in Mexico City, by the mid-1970s these events had also exacted their toll. Only a few ad hoc organizations still existed among the Lahoyan migrants in the capital that still focused primarily on development issues in the home village. One group, made up of old and new enthusiasts of the traza técnica, still gave priority to completing and improving the road leading into the village as the professor had originally envisioned it. Another, and overlapping, group was devoted to the construction of a new schoolhouse. By the end of the decade, both of these projects had bogged down due to continued infighting.

Aftermath

Feelings toward paisanos have persisted among Lahoyans, both in the neighborhoods where they are clustered and in the community at large. From time to time, Lahoyan migrants have tried either to organize or to participate in various groups structured around leisure activities and interests. Examples include musical groups and sundry basketball and soccer teams. Most of these efforts were hampered by participants' work or family schedules. Groups or teams met for some months, but for whatever reason, members often failed to show up regularly enough, and little by little, the migrants complained, things would fall apart. Some commented that unless one worked with paisanos or lived in the same neighborhood with them, life in Mexico City did not really allow the time or the opportunity to get together on any kind of regular basis.

RALU'AN MIGRANTS: MUTUAL AID, NETWORKS, AND ASSOCIATIONS

One early migrant, Sr. Cruz, remembered well his initial experiences in Oaxaca City in the 1930s, and since we were friends, he was willing to talk with me about them in detail. He recalled that there was never much industry in Oaxaca City; the market and related businesses were the core of the city's economy. At times, work was scarce and it was hard to get a job. I was struck by his comment that just being able to eat well enough was a major consideration in his deciding whether to stay in Oaxaca City or return to Ralu'a. Even if one was employed, the work was often hard and the salary minuscule.

Sr. Cruz also emphasized that people in Oaxaca City could be very cruel. When I asked how and why, he said that it was common practice to be teased and humiliated for not being able to speak Spanish well, for being a "hick" from the sierra, and for being naive. He recounted the case of a compatriot who was teased constantly and treated as a buffoon because his Spanish was so poor. In the end, and in part because of the constant torment he had to endure, this young man was unable to pursue his dreams in Oaxaca City and returned to Ralu'a once again to farm.

There were happier memories too. Sr. Cruz also told me that in the old days his paisanos would get together in the public square (the *zócalo*) in the center of town to meet with each other and talk. They used to buy lemonade or ices because no one had enough money to drink. In these weekly gatherings they exchanged information about employment possibilities. If someone needed a job, there was always a chance that a paisano could give him or her a lead.

Other interviews confirmed that Ralu'an migrants who arrived in Mexico City before 1960 faced serious difficulties in adapting. Between 1940 and the late 1950s, migrants were typically self-sufficient upon arrival in the capital. This was not necessarily by choice but because fellow migrants either were too close to the margin of survival themselves to offer much sustained assistance or because there were too few Ralu'an migrants in any one neighborhood to help share the burden, or both. Because of this, a number of Ralu'ans who migrated before 1960 went through trial periods of adaptation; that is, they went back and forth between the village and the city until they had gained enough experience, confidence, and knowledge of the alternatives to enable a permanent move.

Early migrants who managed to go to Mexico City were pushed into services and tertiary jobs that were not directly related to industrial production because they lacked the skills or experience to obtain employment in the industrial sector. Most occupational experiences during this period involved horizontal movement. Migrants changed jobs, but the unskilled, manual nature of the work remained constant. Many people who came during the initial period reported having difficulty adjusting and making a decent living.

Often the early Ralu'an migrants (mostly men) went through an initial "bachelor" period of adaptation, in which living arrangements were quite varied. Once things stabilized and the men married, household formation in Mexico City, as in Ralu'a was usually based on a nuclear family. The urban households of Ralu'an migrants are a flexible unit, however, and through any given family's domestic cycle, close consanguineal or affinal kin might be taken in if economic, social, or pragmatic conditions warranted it.

In short, the stories I heard from the early migrants to Oaxaca and Mexico City during the 1940s and 1950s reminded me very much of the stories I heard from the Lahoyan migrants from the 1940s to the 1970s. Suffering and hardship marked their transition to urban life.

Mexico City Since 1960

The patterns of initial adjustment for Ralu'an migrants who came to Mexico City between 1960 and 1977 were completely different. These later migrants were often facilitated by established Ralu'an migrants. Temporary lodging was frequently arranged for those who, for occupational or educational reasons, decided to move to the capital. By the middle of the 1960s, jobs could even be obtained through more established migrants, albeit in unskilled manual labor in factories or large businesses. During this period, members of the Ralu'an migrant community were, on the whole, willing to aid new migrants whenever and however possible, within limits. In this fashion, established migrants could protect themselves from unreasonable demands.

There is evidence that facilitation was extended by out-migrants to compatriots from very different socioeconomic levels back in Ralu'a. In the 1960s and 1970s, established migrants in Mexico City often helped new migrants who were from families with much wealthier backgrounds. In fact, access to facilitation became one of the major features determining exactly who decided to leave Ralu'a after 1960.

Facilitation in Mexico City was typically based on the norm of paisanazgo, but ties were also usually reinforced though any one of a number of other possible relationships: kinship, *compadrazgo* (god-parenthood), residential propinquity in the village, or friendship, for example. As in the Lahoyan case, everyone who chose to belong to the migrant community contributed what they could, when they could. There were also a few key individuals and families within the community who were especially well known for having provided generous and repeated advice, facilitation, and aid to their compatriots.

In 1977, I estimated that there were between 400 and 500 migrants from the village of Ralu'a over the age of eighteen in Mexico City, divided into approximately 150 households. By 1979, migrants were still arriving in Mexico City, although in smaller numbers. I also learned for the first time, toward the end of my stay, that anywhere from 50 to 100 Ralu'ans were unaccounted for in the capital. With the exception of two or three cases that involved major crimes or the betrayal of family members, I was not able to determine why these individuals had chosen not to affiliate with their paisanos. The status of many was completely unknown, including whether they were actually residing in Mexico City. In retrospect, the nonparticipation of these individuals in the Ralu'an migrant community did not seem to bother their compatriots. Nor did their noninvolvement negate the fact that, for those who *did* choose to participate, normative standards were enforced, if only by means of community opinion (and gossip) about one's merits and morals, and the tangible threat of noncooperation or refusal to give support.

By the late 1960s, largely because of the practice of occupational facilitation, a good number of the Ralu'an migrants were clustered in five or six occupations. While this situation did not last long, such occupational clustering was clearly the product of chain migration and facilitation between kin and paisanos. Although the rate of industrialization in Mexico City had slowed during the 1950s and then shifted to a capital-intensive orientation in the 1960s, the fact that a number of the early Ralu'an migrants had achieved positions of power permitted later Ralu'an migrants to gain access to occupations linked to the formal sector of the urban economy. By 1977, most of the Ralu'an migrants were in occupations linked to the modern industrial sector of the urban economy or at least had access to the salaries and benefits that such a linkage implies. Many jobs were in industrial manufacturing or primary-materials processing and had been obtained on the basis of facilitation by a fellow migrant.

A partial index of the extent and impact of mutual aid among the Ralu'an migrants can be found by looking at their occupational status, standard of living, and housing. A major finding of my interviews with Ralu'an migrants from 1977 to 1979 was that at least 60 percent of the Ralu'an households had one member who was employed in the formal sector of the urban economy. Many Ralu'an migrants thus had jobs that gave them immediate security and that tied them into the mainstream of Mexican national life. The finding of relative occupational and economic achievement on the part of the Ralu'ans in Mexico City is also supported by additional data on standards of living.[2] First of all, examining the incomes of persons interviewed in 60 cases, 10 heads of independent households earned between the minimum salary and 3,000 pesos a month.[3] Another 38 persons earned between 3,000 and 7,000 pesos a month, and 12 earned between 7,000 and 10,000 pesos. Many of these individuals also belonged to unions at their place of work (often because they were obliged to join), but few had joined any other non-Zapotec groups or associations by the late 1970s.

Almost 60 percent of the migrants interviewed in this sample owned their own housing, the condition of which was good (in 24 cases), or average (in 11 cases).[4] All of the households in this group owned an iron, a radio, and a television; 99 percent had stoves; 90 percent had a phonograph; 77 percent had a refrigerator; 45 percent owned a washing machine and a sewing machine; 30 percent had a car; and 19 percent had a telephone.[5]

Perhaps the key point to emphasize is that many men and women experienced occupational stability or upward mobility as a direct result of belonging to the migrant social network. That is, at least 50 percent of the migrants who came after 1960 obtained jobs through the information and recommendations provided by fellow migrants. The percentage is even higher (I estimate it at 70 to 80 percent), if one considers such facilitation and mutual aid in terms of its impact on households rather than on individuals. This was especially the case whenever Ralu'an workers were involved in union activities at businesses where fifteen or more migrants from Ralu'a or the Rincón were employed. For the most part, then, by the end of the 1970s the Ralu'ans were in occupations that were linked to the modern industrial sector of the urban economy, and most had access to the benefits that such a linkage implied.

Beyond the level of households and families, the most significant dimension of migrant social organization had to do with social networks. Like the "reciprocity networks" described by Lomnitz (1977:131–35, 156–58), such networks do not revolve around a particular person. Rather, each participant interacts equally with all the others. Among the Ralu'ans, the bases of such networks include (1) kinship ties (which can be reinforced by propinquity in a common neighborhood or weakened by physical distance); (2) compadrazgo; (3) friendship; (4) a common workplace; and (5) common interests. Often these bases are combined and expressed as relationships between paisanos. In any case, relationships are reinforced by visiting, the exchange of gifts, and the usually implicit promise of solidarity in times of trouble. The exchange of information (and less often, financial resources) may also take place.

Although these networks are characterized by sex, age, and migrant cohorts, membership in them is cross-cutting to a degree. This means that, because of a multiplicity of links and ties, an individual or family may be eligible for membership in a number of networks at the same time, though in most cases individuals give their identity and loyalty to one network over the others. It is also important to note here that married women with children may have less access to networks that operate outside of their immediate neighborhood. Finally, sociability is a major aspect of these networks, and exchange of small items or favors is common among members.

In short, the formation of reciprocity networks followed the creation of informal networks of facilitation between kin and paisanos. Initially these networks were crucial for urban adaptation. The aid, skills, and advice of fellow migrants were often the only resources that new migrants could draw upon. Today, when large numbers of migrants are established in their own jobs and homes, reciprocity networks continue to tie the Ralu'ans together but now at a somewhat more selective "social" level.

As previously indicated, permeating the different relationships among Ralu'an migrants are the many exchanges between migrant individuals and households based on mutual aid and reciprocity. Relatives, friends from village days, and leaders in the Ralu'an community could all be approached for a wide range of assistance. Besides the aid given to new migrants or the exchange that characterizes ongoing reciprocity networks, other relationships that involve mutual aid occur over the long term. Among Ralu'ans in Mexico City, mutual aid tends to be informal, yet it is an important aspect of social relations.

Mutual aid occurs with great frequency in the context of social events. Rites of passage are very important to the Ralu'ans. They relish marking major life events and transitions with celebrations. Birthday celebrations (which are actually celebrations of saint's days), graduations, weddings, and *quince años* celebrations (for young women who have turned fifteen) are extensively planned and often entail great effort and cost. Many relatives and friends are invited, and large quantities of food and drink are prepared and served, all of which involves much purchasing, preparation, and cooking (especially with traditional dishes such as *mole*). Thus the help and participation of female relatives and friends is very desirable.

Sociability is very strong among Ralu'ans. Visiting, which can be difficult and quite time-consuming, given the size of Mexico City, is appreciated and valued. Small gifts may be exchanged during such visits, and a drink and meal are always offered by the hosts. In this fashion, migrants cultivate those persons or families that they most enjoy or that they believe will be good friends and potential allies in times of difficulty or need, whether in the capital or back home in Ralu'a.

Mutual aid is also given in situations of crisis or emergency, although it is entirely on a voluntary and ad hoc basis. By the late 1970s, large open meetings were held only in a few exceptional cases in which an emergency had implications for the entire group. (One such meeting, for example, was held when a young Ralu'an woman was murdered.) More typical were cases involving such events as an accident, sudden or extreme illness, a funeral or an arrest.

Another aspect of mutual aid is that given by migrants to the home village back in Oaxaca. Among the Ralu'ans, ad hoc committees are usually formed, with each in charge of a specific project. Once the project is over, the committee disbands. No officials are elected, and, in fact, legitimacy is gained through confirmation by the village government. When the village government feels the need for input from the migrants, this is communicated to select individuals who carry prestige and influence among the migrants. These individuals spread the word, and in this fashion, candidates for a committee are identified. Projects in the village, such as roads, electrification, piped water, schools, and a new health center have all been carried out with the political, financial, and moral support of the Ralu'an migrants in Oaxaca City and Mexico City. One example of how this process operates occurred in November 1977 when the municipal authorities of Ralu'a called a meeting in Mexico City to discuss three new village projects with out-migrants: a technical high school, a health center, and improvements on the road. The meeting was scheduled for 4:00 P.M. at a private college where one of the Ralu'an migrants was employed as a teacher. As it turned out, the meeting started at around 6:00. In the beginning there were between forty-five and fifty people in attendance, and at its peak, later in the evening, the gathering had grown to between sixty and seventy persons.

The order of events was as follows. The principal of the private college was introduced first, followed by the three municipal authorities who had come from Ralu'a: the president, the *síndico,* and the treasurer. The Ralu'an teacher from the college made the introductions and reminded those gathered that the help and support of each and every one was needed. Then the president took over, thanked everyone for coming, and stated the purpose of the meeting. At this point he stopped and asked for someone in attendance to serve as secretary and take minutes for the meeting. A vote was called for and held, and one of the young women was duly appointed to the task.

The president then mentioned that the committee running the fiesta of the town's patron saint, San José, wanted to do an especially good job that year, so all in attendance were invited to send their contributions to the municipal authorities.

Next, he and the treasurer outlined the plans for each of the three projects. Improvements on the road into Ralu'a were discussed first. Progress was being made, with the hope of completing the work by January of the following year. Machinery and technical assistance were being supplied jointly by the Comisión de Papaloapan and the lumber company, Papelería de Tuxtepec. For their part, the citizens of Ralu'a were cooperating by supplying constant tequio labor.

The second project was the public health center. A good site had already been obtained, and cost estimates for the building were about 371,000 pesos. The center was to have twelve beds on two stories. Co-sponsored by the Comisión de Papaloapan, and the Secretariat of Public Works, the health center was intended to serve the region as a whole.

The third project was the Escuela Tecnológica Agropecuaria (essentially a technically oriented agricultural high school). Again, a site had been obtained for the new buildings, this time up on a hill overlooking Ralu'a, since this was the only place near enough to the village that was both flat enough and open enough for the new facility. This project was to be carried out with government support as well, with costs projected at 212,000 pesos.

Discussion then focused on how payment for these three projects could best be obtained. Since three basic items were needed to complete the latter two projects—sand, gravel, and labor—one proposal was that a total sum of, say, 1,000 pesos should be contributed in partial payments over the course of a year. This proposition caused a burst of spontaneous conversation. Questions were raised: Was the road really going to be paved, or was it still going to be rough? Why didn't the municipal authorities write up a formal document listing all the pertinent facts and figures? Why was Ralu'a selected as the site of these buildings instead of some other community? These questions were answered, and then the treasurer reintroduced the question of payment. In Ralu'a, it turned out, quotas were being paid according to a sliding scale within a four-level hierarchy. Those who were well-off paid the first-level rate of 1,000 pesos, the second paid 750, the third 500, and the fourth 300. It was emphasized that the fourth level was only for those people who had been in Ralu'a for five years or less.

There was much discussion about what each of these levels implied for the residents in Mexico City and how partial payments could be handled. Then there was a short break because the municipal authorities requested some time for a private discussion to resolve the questions and issues that had been raised. When the break ended and the meeting began again, one individual suggested that a total cost projection be made so that the Ralu'ans in Mexico City could agree to raise a certain percentage of this figure. The treasurer took some more time out to confer with his fellow officials and then reported that quotas were computed for one year at a time, with the understanding that it would take some three years for the projects to be completed. The quotas for the health center and the high school were 1,535, 1,450, 1,366, or 1,500 pesos, for example, depending on one's socioeconomic position. The municipio, it turned out, had only general estimates of costs tied to what proportion of each of these figures was to be spent on sand, gravel, labor, and other things.

Variations on this theme were then suggested by members of the audience. One person proposed that a minimum quota be set for all to pay and that those who were able to give more could always opt to do so. Another proposal was that the quota should not be paid by the family head alone but by each member of the household who was over eighteen and employed. After much discussion and debate, a vote was taken on whether the quota should be paid per household or per working member of a given household. The vote was overwhelmingly in favor of a quota of 500 pesos for each working member of the family (or, when relevant, household). Many thanks were immediately expressed by the municipal authorities for this decision.

Next, there was discussion over how the quotas were to be paid. It was decided that a list should be circulated to the entire population of Ralu'ans in Mexico City—some 150 household heads, 200 youths, and an undetermined number of persons (estimated at between 50 and 100) whose presence and status needed to be assessed. It was proposed that circulars first be written and distributed. Then the people appointed to contact fellow workers in a particular job or field would make sure everyone knew about the quota and would proceed to collect the money.

Finally, another meeting was proposed, two weeks later, to plan a future fund-raising event. The hope was to generate more money and either to give this money to Ralu'a or use it as a general fund for further activities.

About two weeks later, I decided to attend the follow-up meeting to see what comments came up about the last session and to find out about the fundraiser. When I arrived a little before 5:00 P.M., the time when the meeting was supposed to start, hardly anyone was there. I went out to get a snack with some friends, which was good, because the meeting did not start until 7:00. This meeting was much smaller than the earlier one, fluctuating between twenty and thirty people as the evening wore on.

The decision to ask for a quota of 500 pesos per working member of each family or household to support two of the three current community projects in Ralu'a was reviewed and the collection procedure for the money was reiterated. Someone expressed concern about the fact that the municipal authorities in Ralu'a had never bothered to (formally or informally) inform folks back home about the decision that had been reached in Mexico City. This news caused some grumbling, but it was conjectured that if the aid from Mexico City were taken for granted by the townsfolk, this might affect their desire to continue working on their own.

Discussion about the fund-raiser focused on throwing a dance for the Ralu'ans in Mexico City. Much time was spent on logistics, including where and when to hold the dance and how to raise the capital needed to get the project off the ground. First it was decided to search for a venue that was reasonably priced and centrally located. Three people were selected to investigate this matter. December 10 was selected as the tentative date. Finances were a major consideration, since—between the dance hall, the band, utilities, and refreshments—people estimated that a total of 16,000 pesos was going to be needed. Some money from the previous dance was available, however, and selected participants were asked to lend the rest of the capital needed on a short-term, no-interest basis.

The last question involved ticket prices. Instead of charging high prices, which was originally proposed but then rejected since it was believed that this would discourage attendance, tickets were set at 50 pesos for women and 60 for men. The difference was to be made up by charging 30 pesos for table seating. A third meeting was set up for a week later, and everyone vowed to come on time.

In summary, mutual aid, like facilitation and reciprocity, is frequent and ongoing in the contemporary Ralu'an migrant community. The bulk of interactions are informal, and while migrants feel impelled to help one another, assistance can be terminated at any point when a burden becomes too onerous or if there is any suspicion that one is being imposed upon. The major exception to this rule involves cooperation with municipal projects back in Ralu'a. Those who do not cooperate earn a bad name back home and may be subject to direct sanctions if they are landowners or if they return home for a visit.

Formal Ralu'an Migrant Associations

Ralu'an migrants have never tried to organize a formal association at the level of the village itself. Rather, two different sets of Ralu'an migrants have been active at two separate times in the organization of regional-level migrant associations.

The first, named the Regional Zapotec Association, was formed with representatives from ten villages in the Rincón and thus involved only Mountain Zapotec migrants who also spoke Nexitzo. The association was formally convened with a constitution and officers in 1960. Its platform focused on the general social and economic improvement of the villages in the Rincón. At that time, each of the villages had its own association, which in turn sent representatives to the larger group.

In the process of organizing the association and holding the initial meetings, the Ralu'an leadership set as its main priority the establishment of a health center somewhere in the Rincón (not to be confused with the Ralu'an health center mentioned above, which was built much later). The leaders believed that, in addition to improving the quality of health services, such a center would promote better communications with and ties to state-level offices. Because a number of its founders were employed in the federal bureaucracy, the association was able to make contact with influential federal officials, including the distinguished Mexican anthropologist and Zapotec specialist Dr. Julio de la Fuente. Members of the association worked hard to promote their cause both by means of these contacts and through contacts with officials in the key Rincón municipalities. In the end, however, the project failed, and the health center was built outside of the area.

According to a number of former officers of the regional association, a number of factors combined to defeat the project, including a lack of enthusiastic response at the grass-roots level and infighting among the Regional Zapotec Association leaders, each of whom was trying to get the center located in his own village. Moreover, as intragroup struggles intensified, leaders and association members called on local politicians from the state of Oaxaca to intervene in the ensuing debates and conflicts.[6] Unfortunately, after this setback in 1963 the Regional Zapotec Association went into a recess from which it has never been able to emerge.

Although the association's health-center project was not successful, a number of important precedents were established. First, the core of Ralu'an migrants involved in this organization centered around men who had come to Mexico City during the first, difficult period of migration. In other words, by 1960 these men had established themselves sufficiently to allow them to take a leadership role in migrant affairs and to become involved in development projects back home. Second, the association was the first group with a formal charter and body of officers that involved a number of villages at a regional level (as opposed to the level of individual village associations). In addition, the migrants made an effort to establish direct ties to the village governments back home in the Rincón.

A second formal association, named the Union of Zapotec Villages, was organized in the early 1970s. It had generally the same platform as the Regional Zapotec Association, but it included representatives from many more villages distributed over two districts of the Sierra Juárez. The major activity of the union was ostensibly to raise money for regional development by giving large dances at which drinks and regional foods were on sale. At the same time, the actual functions of this association cannot be separated from its history: it was organized by a Ralu'an migrant (with the help of members of his extended family) who was an important official in the union at a business that employed many migrants from, but not limited to, the Rincón and the Sierra Juárez, including many of the villages in the district of Villa Alta. When politics arose in the workplace, the Zapotec workers would rally around their paisano and generate support for him or for his position. Thus it appears that this association was primarily oriented toward the migrants and their social and economic needs in the urban setting. In turn, there were those who said that the union official hoped to use his work and associational bases to launch a campaign for a seat as an elected deputy in the state legislature of Oaxaca.

Activities sponsored by the Union of Zapotec Villages came to an end in 1975 when politics at the workplace began to reach a point of crisis and all association activities were suspended. The union official had come under fire from Sr. Fidel Velásquez, the chief of all the official unions in the nation. There was an extended struggle, which was eventually resolved, but the whole affair was so extensive and involved that it ended the official's active participation in the regional association, as well as his immediate hopes for a larger role in Mexican politics.

By the time I left the field, the number of Ralu'ans working in this business had gradually dwindled from about forty persons to about fifteen. Nonetheless, employment opportunities at the business, made available through relationships of paisanazgo and patronage, had provided a solid foundation that many families from Ralu'a and the sierra were able to build upon in Mexico City.

Conclusion

By the late 1970s, the predominant characteristic of the Ralu'an migrants in the capital was their facility at obtaining jobs in, or connected to, the formal sector of the urban economy. Especially after 1960, the initial stages of urban adaptation for migrants were based on extended networks of facilitation and mutual aid.

Formal associations organized by the migrants from Ralu'a have always been on a larger scale than just the village itself. Although Ralu'an migrants developed and organized both of these associations and have always held the key positions, the stated rationale of both groups has always been support for the villages or the region of origin rather than the migrants themselves. In both cases, associational activities bogged down after a relatively brief period.

Ironically, by the end of the 1970s I sensed that the occupational attainments of the Ralu'ans in Mexico City had allowed them to detach themselves gradually from fellow migrants for all practical purposes if they so chose. Concomitantly, over time, occupational diversity among the migrants may have also curtailed their ability to engage in broad collective responses or actions.

One Ralu'an migrant volunteered an interesting comment toward the end of my stay. He claimed that the Ralu'an associations had not always worked well. They had not been scrupulous in their handling of monies, and the personal goals and egos of the leadership sometimes got mixed up with the aims of the group as a whole. Despite these drawbacks, this out-migrant claimed, there was a real need for Ralu'ans to stick together and even to have an association to speak for them and act in their common interest.

I can say little about those Ralu'ans in Mexico City who chose not to affiliate with their paisanos. Moreover, in the course of eighteen months of interviews with Ralu'ans over a period of five years, I received only two or three critical statements from people who maintained that one could not expect any solid advice or aid from paisanos and/or that the community as a whole had not been able to benefit from ties of paisanazgo between individuals or families. In fact, the person whom I remember being especially vehement about the fact that he could not depend on anyone was in fact the recipient of a good deal of moral and tangible aid from his extended family (who freely acknowledged to me that their relative was a somewhat cantankerous individual). The lack of interest and involvement expressed by these few, however, represents sentiments that were clearly shared by others.

VILLALTECO OUT-MIGRANTS

From time to time during my two-year stay in Mexico City I heard rumors about migrants from Villa Alta. One migrant from the district seat told me about a Villalteco migrant association called the Comité Villalteco, which had a formal board of directors. I was told that the organization held fund-raisers and was interested in offering economic help in the development of the district. The few informal interviews I was able to conduct suggested that the four hundred or so migrants from Villa Alta were one of the largest of the Mountain Zapotec communities in Mexico City and perhaps the largest in proportion to the population of the village of origin.

The outstanding characteristic of these migrants was the extent to which they were occupationally concentrated in the state bureaucracy, especially in jobs related to the Mexican telegraph and postal services, as well as in the primary levels of the teaching profession. One migrant (who was not from Villa Alta but who associated with the community), estimated that well over 50 percent of the Villalteco out-migrant families had at least one member working in one of these three fields. The same individual, however, acknowledged that at least 20 percent of the Villaltecos were working for minimal wages or simply selling wage labor on a day-to-day basis.

Although a recent account by Parnell (1988) focuses mainly on the town and the immediate region of origin, he presents some fascinating data regarding Villalteco out-migrants, which can be outlined here. Parnell notes that, generally, "[u]rban Villaltecos in Oaxaca City and in Mexico City are organized politically around opposed village political groups, the Caleros and Progressives" (Parnell 1988:11). The urban Calero supporters are reported to be an older, more financially secure, and more tightly organized group than the urban supporters of the Progressives. According to Parnell, the Caleros include a number of influential professionals and bureaucrats in Mexico City and Oaxaca City. The group was particularly active in Oaxaca City, setting up an organization called the Villalteco Cultural Association to support the Calero faction back in the town. The level of security and sophistication of the Caleros in Oaxaca City is partly reflected in the fact that the association "published a book that chronicled the Caleros' role in the construction of the new road. It included copies of their correspondence with state and federal officials" (Parnell 1988:48). To my knowledge, this was the first time a Mountain Zapotec migrant association has gone to such efforts to document their role in a village development project.

As teachers and as operators and office workers in the national telegraph and postal service, many of the urban Progressives are clustered in the same types of occupations that their parents pursued. As organized groups in Oaxaca and in Mexico City, they are opposed to the urban Caleros in the same locales, and, although they are younger and less secure, they support the town's progressive leader, David Mendiolea. Mendiolea's group focuses on development projects in Villa Alta, and the urban Progressives support such projects morally and financially. Because their zeal extended to both general fund-raising and individual donations, Mendiolea expressed his firm faith in these out-migrants as "responsible villagers" (Parnell 1988:56).

The urban progressives also facilitate the political connections and petitions usually needed in order to win government financial backing. For this reason, the urban migrants constitute an important base of support for Mendiolea and his followers. Parnell notes, however, that as federal and state agencies provided monies for the further development of Villa Alta, "the seat's isolation in the district increased. Regional assemblies and Protestant churches brought organization and new alliances among outlying villagers who opposed both the state and the district seat" (1988:49). Thus the political dynamics of the region have had a direct impact on the motives for creating support groups among urban residents and the solicitation of their moral and monetary support for the causes of the district seat.

Beyond this, the urban residents, Parnell notes, remit money to their families back in Villa Alta on an individual basis but are also quite active in forming committees in Mexico City that support annual village fiestas (Parnell 1988:11). Parnell describes the commitments of the latter kind in terms of the participation of a Mexico City committee's involvement in the *mayordomía* concerning the Santo Entierro in this way:

> One week before the fiesta, representatives of the village's Mexico City committee arrive in Villa Alta. Each year an image of the Santo Intierro [*sic*] is taken from Villa Alta to go from house to house in Oaxaca City or Mexico City. Village urbanites pay their city's village committee for the privilege of hosting the image in their homes. (1988:27–28)

The committee uses funds gathered in this way to support the organization of the Santo Entierro fiesta in subsequent years.

In this fashion, whether they are adherents of the Caleros or the Progressives and whether they have been able to achieve occupational and financial security as individuals or as families, Parnell observed that the out-migrants from Villa Alta in Oaxaca City and Mexico City "continue to participate in the politics, conflicts, disputes, and economy of their native village" (1988:5).

CONCLUSION

Three basic patterns characterize the social and economic organization of the three migrant communities considered above. First of all, it is meaningful to divide the experience of out-migrants into two broad stages. Whether they were from Lahoya or Ralu'a, migrants who went to Mexico City before 1960 generally experienced a difficult period of initial adjustment. Linguistic and cultural patterns played a role here, as did the migrants' unfamiliarity with the city and urban life. Nonetheless, by the late 1970s most of the migrants who had come before 1960 were not distinguishable from their more recent peers in dress, homes, or possessions, yet the experiences of those who were willing to recount their stories to me at length were often marred by initial periods of alienation, suffering, and despair because they experienced prejudice and often exploitation. Admittedly, this experience may not be characteristic of all the early Villalteco migrants, given that some of those who ventured from the town went with better skills and thus were able to pursue stable, secure careers with more ease. In contrast, those migrants who arrived after 1960 were able to draw from a much wider range of paisanos, some of whom were in a position to offer advice, leads, and even jobs. In this climate of support and community, the life histories that I obtained suggested much less trauma and much more personal and collective confidence despite the inevitable difficulties.

Second, while the vast majority of the Lahoyan and Ralu'an out-migrants during the pre-1960 period were relegated to being servants or selling wage labor on a daily basis, with no benefits and little or no occupational security, the migrants who came after 1960 had the opportunity to obtain skilled or semiskilled jobs in the formal, industrialized sectors of the job market. In an urban economic setting in which, although growth had slowed, the job market was still expanding, personal ties of paisanazgo were a perfect mechanism to recruit new, reliable workers since established workers could (and did) recommend, train, and generally guarantee their compatriots. Consequently, during the 1970s many men and women from Ralu'a, and an increasing number of Lahoyan men, obtained access to jobs that were in the formal sector of the economy and reaped the tangible benefits, including good wages, at least some job security, and access to goods and services, including subsidized housing developments.

Despite these improvements, a qualitative analysis of the data indicates that even in the comparatively ideal setting of the 1960s and 1970s, migrants' jobs, promotions, salaries, and security were very much framed by the educational and economic opportunities available in the communities of origin. Not surprisingly, then, the Lahoyans—whose exposure to Spanish was limited, whose educational levels were also limited, and whose occupational experiences revolved primarily around self-provisioning agricultural pursuits—generally faced more difficulties in finding and sustaining decent employment than either the majority of the Ralu'ans or the Villaltecos.

PART III

Interpretations

CHAPTER 7

Ethnographic Analysis

Since the capital city of many Latin American nations, including Mexico, has been the primary site of industrial development since World War II, occupational and educational opportunities have abounded there, especially compared to those available in the countries' secondary urban centers. Thus, Mountain Zapotec out-migrants often choose the capital as the main urban point of destination. Ties involving kinship, friendship, and common origin—all of which are wrapped up in the Mountain Zapotec migrants' concept of paisanazgo—have provided the foundation for a pattern of chain migration to Mexico City. The subsequent facilitation of new migrants has led to common occupations and/or class situations, as well as initial patterns of residential concentration.

As we have seen most clearly among the Ralu'ans in Mexico City, Mountain Zapotec migrants from Oaxaca who regard each other as paisanos affiliate with each other on the basis of at least seven forms of behavior that are based on common origin: (1) pursuing a shared lifestyle, customs, food preferences, religious beliefs and practices, and in most cases, language; (2) exchanging benefits based on reciprocity and mutual aid; (3) visiting, having parties, and celebrating rites of passage; (4) pursuing hobbies or special interests such as sports or music; (5) facilitating the acquisition of jobs and housing; (6) creating networks based on a common workplace; and (7) establishing migrant associations. In general, informal uses of regional culture along the lines of points 1 through 5 are adaptive and efficacious. This may be because they are egalitarian and inherently voluntary. Although ties based on, and carried out in terms of, paisanazgo can be and sometimes are subject to abuse, they can be terminated fairly easily in the situations described in points 1 through 5, which helps to protect the provider of support. In addition, among all the groups considered here, the migrant communities have made use of informal aspects of paisanazgo to enhance their members' primary interactions and the quality of their lives in the capital.

At a more instrumental and material level, facilitation appears to be quite effective in occupational placement, albeit within certain limits. Migrants' initial jobs and their subsequent occupational trajectories tend to reflect the levels of education and opportunity available in the point of origin. This is most clearly illustrated in the case of the Villalteco migrants, whose clustering in professions related to teaching, the postal service, and telecommunications reflects specializations that could be learned if not practiced in the town itself.

The introduction to this book raised a question that can now be addressed more systematically: Given all the alternatives for alliance that are available to them, why would Mountain Zapotec migrants select common origin as a basis for identity and emphasize a norm of paisanazgo as the basis for urban solidarity and mutual aid? Part of the answer to this question lies in the fact that the idea of common origin is an attempt to build from what migrants have—namely, their paisanos—to get what they need, either individually or collectively. In the urban setting, where a sense of rural communal solidarity is reactivated and transformed to meet the day-to-day challenges of city life, the idea of common origin is selected as a rationale for individual interaction and group organization because it provides the basis for migrant cooperation at three interrelated levels.

First, common origin provides a significant criterion for delineating kith and kin as potential allies. Once their kith and kin are defined as such, migrants have a fairly clear basis for identifying and recruiting a larger body of participants who are distinctive (see Cohen 1969:201–5) and who can be easily recruited through an individual's family or network ties. By contrast, if Mountain Zapotecs engaged in alliance and reciprocity solely on the basis of kinship, their field of social relations would be much narrower than the more flexible concept of paisano provides them.

Second, the idea of common origin is a desirable basis for organizing migrant social relations in that it implies common values that help in establishing and meeting common objectives and goals, whether these are directed toward the point of origin or toward fellow migrants in the city. In this sense, common origin has a religious dimension throughout much of Latin America. A number of studies of Mexican communities, for example, make reference to a strong spiritual unity symbolized by the church as the center of the town and its residents (e.g., Foster 1960:34, 48; Hunt and Nash 1967:268–72;

Simpson 1971:101–4). The cemetery as the final resting place of the community's deceased is another expression of spiritual unity, and older migrants expressed a strong preference to be buried back in Ralu'a, not in the capital. These points are of special importance in a huge urban agglomeration like Mexico City, which is filled with strangers whose values and practices are undetermined if not unknowable.

Third, entailed in the notion of common origin is the assumption that paisanos will be willing and able to work together precisely because of a shared cultural and social background. In short, from an individual migrant's point of view, ties based on shared origin can offer a basis for trust and a greater possibility of action to promote individual and collective interests and commitments, both ideally and in reality, compared to the populace at large. Specifically, when Mountain Zapotecs find themselves in a megalopolis such as Mexico City, where they are at a disadvantage—sometimes an extreme disadvantage—in competing for jobs and other resources, paisanazgo provides a familiar context and a means for obtaining provisions, information, resources, and political power. This is probably most true in the early stages of the migrants' lives in the city, when they share a similar position at the lower levels of the urban system of social stratification. Mountain Zapotec migrants thus emphasize solidarity even though their actual social relations are often dyadic and individualistic. The emphasis derives from the fact that migrants initially face many disadvantages in adapting to urban life—disadvantages that are framed by structural conditions in the points of origin and in the point destination. In this light, even if its invocation is only rhetorical at times, paisanazgo helps pave the way for alliances and actions to combat conditions and circumstances that might otherwise crush the isolated migrant.

Finally, at each of these levels, the Mountain Zapotec migrant case studies confirm the analysis of Francesca M. Cancian that norms "define identities that are located in groups or institutions," and that norms, as "collective perceptions of identities," tend to be reflected in actions (Cancian 1975:158, an analysis that contrasts with that offered by Homans [see chap. 2, n. 2]).

CONDITIONS THAT FRAME THE APPEARANCE OF PAISANAZGO IN MEXICO CITY

Among the Mountain Zapotec migrants I studied, the following conditions framed the selection and use of regional forms of identity entailed in the norm of paisanazgo. First, there is often an orientation toward local levels of identification (i.e., pueblismo) in the community or region of origin.[1] Beyond explicit statements, or *dichos* (sayings), possible indexes of pueblismo in the provincial setting include a tradition of civic or communal labor on behalf of the community, as well as endogamous marriage patterns. Second, the evolution of patterns of chain migration, and the facilitation this implies, allows for the recomposition of groups whose members are bound by sentiments and practices tied to regional identity in the urban setting. Third, an open, if not expanding, employment market with a continuing demand for new laborers appears to facilitate the overall process. In the Mountain Zapotec cases, jobs were available at skilled and semiskilled levels and were often attached, directly or indirectly, to the formal sector of the job market. This also helped to intensify migration to Mexico City during the 1960s and 1970s, in that Ralu'ans came to the capital knowing that they could get a job in a specific company or business and join a union, fully aware of the fact that unions were commonly used by the Mexican government to channel resources like housing to the urban working class. Finally, there must be a sufficient number of migrants in the point of destination to create a large enough network to be of use. I hesitate to identify an exact number, since propinquity and other situational variables play a role here.[2] This point, however, became evident when visiting Ralu'an migrants in Los Angeles in the early 1980s. While the heads of some fifteen to twenty Ralu'an households knew about each other, and visiting and socializing took place among some of them, there did not appear to be tight bonds of reciprocity and exchange among the Ralu'ans in Los Angeles compared to their compatriots in Mexico City. In short, although comparative perspectives on regional identities in urban settings suggest that this need not always be the case (e.g., Weisser 1985), paisanazgo blossomed among the Mountain Zapotecs in Mexico City after 1960, when more than 200 out-migrants from a given community were living there and when both occupational and community resources, as well as government-initiated development programs, were at a peak.

These variables, which span and encompass the points of origin and destination, also help to explain why migrants from Lahoya and Villa Alta during the period I studied manifested such a strong norm of paisanazgo in Oaxaca City and Mexico City even though their communities in the sierra manifested less of a commitment to, and actual involvement in, formal and informal associations than did those in Ralu'a.

The available literature indicates the salience of similar variables and processes in numerous indigenous peasant communities in contemporary Oaxaca. Mention of paisanazgo among out-migrants similar to the ones I have studied appears in brief reports concerning Zapotec migrants from such sierran communities as Lachirioag, Zoogocho, and Copa Bitoo (see Parnell 1988:10–11, 76–80; Berg 1974:229; Young 1976), among the Valley Zapotec in the case described by Dennis (1976:54–55) and among the Isthmus Zapotec (Covarrubias 1946:160–61, 300–301). Sentiments of pueblismo back home and of paisanazgo among out-migrants have also been documented among the neighboring Mixtec (see Butterworth 1962:261, 263; Mendez y Mercado 1985: 199–200; Kearney 1986; and Cederström 1989 and 1990). The French anthropologist Marta Romer provides a corollary account of out-migrants in Mexico City from the Mixe community of Totontepec (Romer 1982:98–99, 112–29).[3] Similar phenomena are widely reported among indigenous peasants throughout Latin America (see Altamirano and Hirabayashi, forthcoming).

A REEVALUATION OF HYPOTHESES ON MIGRANT ASSOCIATIONS

Now that we have discussed paisanazgo, it is appropriate to ask whether the migrant associations were indeed formed to fulfill any of the three broad functions discussed in Chapter 2: (1) to ease sociocultural transitions, (2) to gain control of scarce resources, or (3) to address the manifestations of structurally generated inequities back home. In terms of the cultural perspective, which is predicated on the idea of a transition from the countryside to the city, each of the Zapotec migrant associations did help to orient newcomers and make them secure, but the associations apparently did not help migrants bridge the gap between the language and culture they had known in their village and that which they experienced on moving to the capital. It is notable that much of this immediate function appears to have been carried out between dyads of individuals, between new migrants as individuals and established migrant families, or in the context of informal networks. In this sense, the Mountain Zapotec associations discussed here did not impede the migrants' articulation or integration with either individuals or institutions in the larger society.

The data suggest that migrant associations were only partially effective with respect to resource competition. Whether they came earlier or later, Mountain Zapotec migrants generally operated from a position of relative material scarcity during their initial years of adjustment. Again, dyadic relationships and/or reciprocity networks usually met such needs (except in the case of emergency), and Mountain Zapotec associations apparently have never dealt directly and collectively with issues of material provisioning in their urban communities at large.

On the other hand, the second Ralu'an regional association provides an interesting example of the advancement and protection of special interests, framing the expression of what might be called a "politicized ethnicity." Remember that the leadership and the core membership of the Union of Zapotec Villages was closely tied to a large enterprise where many Zapotec were employed. Thus, Jongkind's emphasis on the uses of migrant associations by and for a small migrant elite is probably an appropriate interpretive tool for some cases. At its peak, however, the union clearly played an important role in the Mountain Zapotec migrant community; many newcomers were placed in jobs through its offices, although of course they then had to engage in political organizing and action in support of their *patrón* and his group in the factory. Because the union's leadership also had ties to the Confederación de Trabajadores Mexicanos (CTM), a number of families eventually gained access to subsidized housing, which was available to Mexico's urban working class at an excellent price. It can be argued, in opposition to Jongkind's hypothesis, that this setup benefited all the parties involved and that although the association was initiated by an elite within the community, it could not have been carried out without the cooperation of everyone (including the poorest of the new migrants, many of whom were grateful for whatever initial employment they could obtain). Similarly, the majority of those involved, whatever their class position, reaped benefits—both material benefits and less tangible but no less valuable benefits, including the symbolic capital that accrued to those who helped others (see Campbell 1990).

From the structural perspective, it is significant that each of the migrant associations emphasized the development of the home village or region. While nostalgia provided the motive for the involvement of some, others, notably community leaders and students, explicitly articulated concern over the underdevelopment of the provinces compared to Mexico's cities, especially the capital, and thus their commitment to improving their home community's infrastructure.

The case studies reveal that each of the Mountain Zapotec communities organized its associations at about the same time and, at least rhetorically, in response to structural issues of underdevelopment. On this basis, Mountain Zapotec migrant associations have generally played a progressive role both in the points of origin and destination. This is not to say that the contributions of migrant associations to their village or region of origin are universally accepted or acknowledged; often they are not, or their significance is downplayed at home. In some cases, outright resistance develops, as it did among the leading families in Lahoya toward the professor and his group. At any rate, I found no indication that the Villaltecos or the Ralu'ans (whether in the Villa Alta district or in Mexico City) saw the Lahoyans' efforts as a threat or ever tried to intervene in or otherwise block the implementation of the Lahoyans' goals or projects.

Class divisions within the Mountain Zapotec associations have been muted during the period under consideration (with the possible exception of the Lahoyan case). In any event, conflicts within migrant associations have tended to dissolve overall group solidarity, at least among the Lahoyans and Ralu'ans, rather than dividing participants along explicit class lines (cf. Kemper 1988). The Villaltecos apparently suspend internal divisions and will work together in defense of their town if it is threatened. In short, class segments *within* the migrant communities discussed here have not organized themselves as a group or reached out to non-Zapotecs in common cause (with the possible exception of a few progressive student workers, who have acted as individuals more than as Zapotecs or representatives of Zapotec groups per se).

AN ETHNOGRAPHIC ANALYSIS OF THE MOUNTAIN ZAPOTEC MIGRANT ASSOCIATIONS

Beyond the factors cited above, what helps to explain the different forms that these group's migrant associations have taken in terms of size, organization and focus? What factors have influenced the efficacy of migrant associations, including their tendency to engage in factionalism and conflict?

To begin to answer these questions, we must return to the observation that each of the communities of origin studied represents a different position in the overall regional hierarchy of sociocultural integration (Wolf 1967:229). As the district seat, Villa Alta is a financial and commercial center, as well as the district seat for the state judicial system. Ralu'a, as the key marketing center of the Rincón, is increasingly linked to outside market forces and is increasingly unable to maintain a self-provisioning status. Lahoya, although it experienced a "boom and bust" cycle during the 1950s, is a remote agricultural village in the hinterlands of the Ralu'an marketing district. Taking these characteristics into account, it is perhaps not surprising that the migrants in Mexico City from each of these communities are organized somewhat differently and that the focus of their migrant associations varies.

The Lahoyan migrants' urban social relations have often been dedicated to helping fellow migrants, and developing Lahoya for, as they said, "the good of the entire pueblo." Especially in their case, what is striking about the strength and the range of their urban facilitation and mutual aid is that such an emphasis is not apparent in the rural setting. Thus, mutual aid among indigenous peasant migrants in Latin American cities is not always a direct transfer of a rural communal orientation but can instead be a reflection of the fact that the city presents such an overwhelming set of challenges, especially in the beginning, that rural migrants prefer to face it in alliance with each other rather than individually. Similarly, in the rural sphere the Villaltecos are generally perceived as aggressively distinguishing themselves on the basis of their "Spanish" origins in contradistinction to the surrounding indigenous communities. Yet Villalteco migrants in both Oaxaca and Mexico City continue to visit the town, form support committees for various town fiestas and projects, and even form migrant village associations, just like their supposedly more indigenous neighbors.

The Ralu'an migrants typically are proud of their town but have chosen to organize formally at the regional and pan-sierran levels. Interestingly enough, this is a manifestation of ethnic identity that is distinct from any I ever heard articulated in Ralu'a itself during the 1970s, and in the conclusion I identify some of the dynamics that suggest that broader ethnic coalitions will be an important trend among the rural and urban populations of indigenous peasants from Oaxaca in the 1990s.

What is most striking in all three cases, however, is that the process of forming migrant associations appears to be inseparably linked to the regional development policies pursued by the Mexican government. As we have already seen, ever since the Mexican Revolution, regional development in regard to indigenous peoples has been based on an integrationist approach spearheaded by the federal government. On the assumption that the modernization and economic integration of the hinterlands with the larger nation would be the best way to ensure the entrance of Mexico's Indians into the larger society and polity, many economic and sociocultural programs directed toward "culture change" (read assimilation) were implemented following the Mexican Revolution. As described in Chapter 3, the concrete manifestations of this policy in the highlands of Oaxaca have had a long and complex history. It is ironic that government-supported programs of regional development between 1950 and 1980 were supposed to address uneven development and also to promote a sense of *national* identity in the rural hinterlands. Instead, the development programs appear initially to have intensified village-level identity both in the Rincón and among the region's out-migrants. Thus the fact that, as de la Fuente has said, "every Zapotec village has a clear view of itself as superior to all other villages" (1965:31), was further exacerbated as each community competed to win the benefits of federal and state programs. In the urban setting, the corollary of this process arose as the migrants supported (or in the Lahoyan case, initiated) such efforts and presented petitions to government officials requesting support and the resources needed to bring "progress" to their communities of origin.

Thus the formation of regional migrant associations in Mexico City occurred in the context of the government's efforts to develop and incorporate the rural hinterlands into the contemporary nation. Specifically, the precise form that migrant associations take appears to have a great deal to do with the power structures, in both the provinces and the city, that frame them.[4] Of special importance in this regard are (1) the political organization of the home village vis-à-vis the broader region of origin; (2) the political organization of the migrants in the urban setting; and, (3) the articulation of 1 and 2 in terms of who ultimately controls the activities and goals of a given migrant association, whether formed at the village or regional level.

Lahoyan migrants in Mexico City, for example, came from one of the most limited economic settings in the Rincón. The dearth of educational and occupational alternatives in the village affected the subsequent urban experiences of most Lahoyan out-migrants because their chance of obtaining a good job or moving upward in the socioeconomic structure of the capital were limited even during periods of economic expansion. Given social, cultural, linguistic, and economic barriers to individual upward mobility, the Lahoyans had a strong incentive to stick together as a group in the urban setting.

The Lahoyan migrants' village associations were initiated and controlled by out-migrants. The village of Lahoya was sorely in need of infrastructure in order to begin revitalizing a stagnant economy. A man I have called the professor—a charismatic leader among the migrants who had the knowledge and contacts to obtain and administer federal and state development grants effectively—founded a migrant association dedicated to the development of the home village. He attracted enough dedicated followers to put his vision of development into action, and subsequent events highlight the fact that migrant associations formed and controlled by out-migrants may generate division and factionalism because development projects potentially threaten entrenched political interests in the home village. While present among the migrants from the beginning, such factionalism was exacerbated by the prominent families of Lahoya, who fought tooth and nail to prevent the professor and his followers from completing their version of the road, among other projects. For this same reason, the overall effect of associations on the Lahoyan migrants, not to mention the village itself, was counterproductive.

In the case of Ralu'a, the central issue is how and why formal manifestations of paisanazgo took on a pan-regional thrust during the 1970s, both in the city and the point of origin. To get a handle on this question, let us first attempt to determine why the Ralu'an migrants did not form a village-level association in Mexico City. What variable was missing, so to speak, that discouraged the formation of such an association despite the presence of many favorable conditions—specifically, urban reciprocity networks based on ties of kinship and paisanazgo, and the presence among the out-migrants of strong feelings of loyalty to and nostalgia about Ralu'a?

Both census data and fieldwork indicate that, in the larger context of the district, Ralu'a has had a steady pattern of growth and development. It is basically the economic, political, and cultural center of the Rincón. Power in Ralu'a is centralized in the town's municipal government, and its officials have provided strong, dynamic leadership. Because of this, the town has been able to take advantage of state and federal development programs that have extended infrastructure and modern services into the rural hinterlands. Thus, by the 1970s Ralu'a was one of the most developed communities in the Rincón and the Villa Alta district.

In the urban setting, especially since the 1960s, mutual aid between the Ralu'an migrants has been multidimensional and crucial in the process of adapting to urban life. Still, an orientation toward upward mobility and occupational and educational attainment—all of which were possible (at least in the period under consideration) for migrants with the right educational and cultural background—along with the Ralu'ans' dispersal throughout Mexico

City, made the formation of a village-level association less practical. Instead, informal social and occupational groupings provided the ties that bound the Ralu'ans together.

Once they became established, however, some of the urban Ralu'an leaders tried to exercise a leadership role at a broader regional level among out-migrants from the local marketing area as well as the sierra as a whole. This leadership has had a number of effects. First, although Ralu'an migrants were effectively prevented from playing a development role at the level of the home community, they did compete for development funds at a regional level, in this case the Rincón. This summarizes the organizing principal of the Regional Zapotec Association, the first effort in this regard.

Interestingly enough, the second regional organizing effort coordinated by Ralu'an migrants was closely tied to an urban workers' union in which a good many Mountain Zapotecs and Oaxaqueños participated. While the explicit rationale for this regional association was also rural development, and while a number of fund-raising events and civic improvement projects were indeed carried out, the leaders used the organization to bolster their political and economic fortunes in the urban workplace. This was, of course, a two-way street in the sense that the stronger the position of the union leadership became, the more effectively and efficiently that leadership could obtain resources and distribute them, in a patron–client fashion, to the membership.

Finally, this is an appropriate point at which to emphasize that, despite their relatively rapid and very real achievements in Mexico City, the Ralu'an migrants were by no means committing themselves to wholesale assimilation. At the same time that they were attempting to become as "Mexican" as possible and to enjoy the resources that that status provided, first-generation Ralu'an migrants were not rejecting their own language and cultural heritage. Certainly, while there is variation within this population, as there is in any group, the vast majority of the Ralu'an migrants I met felt at ease with their identity as Ralu'ans, and many spent a good deal of their time off sharing friendships, visits, and leisure activities with their kin and paisanos.

Since its establishment, Villa Alta has been surrounded by less powerful Zapotec peasant villages (de la Fuente 1965:51). Presently the town is confronted with new kinds of political alliances and levels of resistance, including those represented by both regional assemblies and Protestant converts (Mejía Piñeros and Sarmiento Silva 1987; Marroquín 1989). The major forms of political linkage Villaltecos have sought in order to address these challenges have been either (1) ties to the state and the nation established by individual caciques and political brokers, and (2) ties to the Villalteco out-migrants (Parnell 1988). In the latter case, as we have seen, both of the two primary village caciques and their followers cultivated support groups among out-migrants in Oaxaca and Mexico City to bolster their power base. One cacique in particular, David Mendiolea, began to broker development projects in order to create improvements and generate more political support for his group.

Indeed, what is quite notable is the extent to which the formal migrant village associations of the Villaltecos in Oaxaca City and Mexico City are predominantly extensions of the key rural factions. Thus the politicization and much of the direction and thrust of the Villalteco migrant associations appear to derive from village leadership and village political dynamics.

So far the analysis has focused on discovering why and how migrant associations among Mountain Zapotec migrants were formed. Once these questions are answered, other characteristics become much more understandable. The issues of efficacy and persistence, for example, are more amenable to analysis once questions are clarified that have to do with why, by whom, and for whom the migrant associations came into existence.

From this vantage point, the Lahoyan village associations do not seem especially effective, because the positive initiatives and efforts of out-migrants in Mexico City were politically stymied by the power elite back in the home village. In such a situation, it is also not surprising that everyone involved was worn down by the political battling over the years and that by 1975 both associations, whose members were once extremely engaged, were for the most part inactive.

An analysis of why the Ralu'an migrant leaders chose a regional rather than a village level of organization helps to explain why their organizations were neither very effective nor long-lived. Because the first regional association's rural base was weak (and it thus lacked a key rationale for motivating and organizing urban migrants), it could not make an effective contribution to regional development programs and so rather quickly went into decline. The second organization, while ostensibly organized for similar purposes, actually appears to have served the occupational and political needs of the dozens of Ralu'an and Mountain Zapotec migrants who worked in one large urban industry. However, once this association became bogged down in the internal politics of the plant and the possibility of tangible patronage diminished, it, too, began to lose momentum.

Among the Villaltecos in Mexico City, it will be remembered, migrant factionalism in the urban setting is basically a reflection of existing factions in the town. In this case, factionalism seems to have been kept under control in rural and urban settings through the use of *la voz pública* (public opinion) and, failing that, formal and informal techniques for managing disputes, all based on the principle that Villaltecos should retain control over their own affairs. This orientation seems to have prevented the Villaltecos as a whole from falling into the destructive level of conflict that ultimately divided the Lahoyans. Thus, the presence of external threats to the town in the sierra and the community's ability to delimit political competition and rivalry have enabled Villa Alta's leaders to set the direction and scope of the migrant village associations and to make effective use of out-migrants' contributions.

In summary, the form that a given association assumed and its overall effectiveness have had a great deal to do with the general linkages and the dynamics tying together compatriots at the points of origin and destination. These same factors also influence the choice of what key functions a migrant association addresses.

CONCLUSION

Generally speaking, I have argued that, whether looking at paisanazgo or migrant associations, regional ties and norms binding paisanos rather than "Indianness" per se are a key resource for cultural innovation among Mountain Zapotec migrants in Mexico City. Regional ties thus facilitate creative response to both of the paramount challenges facing first-generation out-migrants. The first involves an overwhelming urban environment characterized by limited social services and thus an environment in which individual and collective forms of self-reliance are of great benefit. The other challenge has to do with points of origin that typically require moral and material support from both the government and out-migrants if they are going to broaden their basic infrastructure as well as social services like as education, sanitation, and health.

At the same time, the three communities of Mountain Zapotec out-migrants —those from the district seat, from a marketing center, and from a self-provisioning agricultural village—organized their associations in different ways. Accounting for why each association was created and why it took the form that it did requires an understanding of (1) the larger structural contexts and constraints (2) the ethnography of each community of origin, and (3) the kinds of ties that each migrant community developed and sustained with kith and kin back home in the provinces, with particular attention to the locus of political influence and control.

CHAPTER 8

Conclusion

The purpose of this book is to describe the role of paisanazgo (a norm that emphasizes solidarity among persons from the same locale) in Mountain Zapotec urban life, especially in regard to mutual aid and the formation of migrant associations. Mountain Zapotec migrants in Mexico City engage in such practices, yet their commitment to and manifestations of mutual aid, especially the focus and forms of migrant associations, vary somewhat unexpectedly. In this book I have sought to describe these cases ethnographically and to account for the major variations among them.

The ethnographic overviews presented above focus on out-migrants from three communities in the region of origin, the district of Villa Alta in Oaxaca. These are Villa Alta, the district seat; Ralu'a, a local marketing center; and Lahoya, a self-provisioning agricultural community in the hinterlands. These communities provide an effective sample of local variation, representing as they do three levels of sociocultural integration (see Table 8.1).

Villa Alta is the wealthiest of the three and the most articulated to the state and nation, yet according to Parnell, Villaltecos do practice mutual aid in the pursuit of community solidarity and development. Lahoya is the poorest and currently the most isolated, both internally and externally, in the sense that there is the least mutual aid beyond formal governmental and religious obligations, and the least importing and exporting of products. Ralu'a is well developed, at least by regional standards: the town has a strong infrastructure, including a road; it is the seat of many regional offices of government departments and agencies; and it is a regional marketing center, with all that such a

Table 8.1
Rural and Urban Characteristics of the Three Mountain Zapotec Communities
and Their Out-Migrants in Mexico City, 1980

Community of Origin	Rural Attributes	Urban Attributes
Lahoya	Zapotec-speaking; agricultural village within the Ralu'an marketing system; limited mutual aid	blue-collar; two once-active village associations; factionalism
Ralu'a	bilingual; postconquest settlement; town; local marketing and administrative center; frequent mutual aid	blue- and white-collar; reciprocity networks; two short-lived regional associations;
Villa Alta	Spanish speaking; district seat; district judicial, administrative, and mercantile center encompassing the above communities; some mutual aid	many professionals and white-collar; informal village support committees; active village associations

status implies. Ralu'a is also outstanding in the number of formal and informal mutual-aid groups that cut across the populace and help bind the community together. The three communities manifest different degrees of Zapotec ethnicity, social solidarity, and economic and occupational pursuits, as well as sociopolitical articulation with the Mexican nation.

Patterns of migration from each community have varied over time. Migration from Ralu'a and Lahoya are best divided for analytical purposes into two periods: pre-1960 and 1960 and after. These periods correlate with people's motives for leaving, patterns of migration, and initial experiences in their urban points of destination. While there are interesting similarities in the stated motives for migration and even in broad migration patterns, each community's migrants experienced different rates and kinds of adjustment to life in Mexico City.

The pre-1959 migrants from Lahoya and Ralu'a were either an elite group of scholars and religious students or people who had little or no opportunity for economic improvement in their home communities. The stated motives for migration of the latter typically involved economic hardship, lack of resources, and/or domestic difficulties. Between the 1940s and the late 1950s, migrants generally worked as servants or as wage laborers in Oaxaca City.

Those who wound up in the capital of the state or the nation generally suffered a great deal in their initial years.

Much less detailed information was available on Villa Alta, so it is not clear at this point whether the two-period approach to out-migration is fully applicable to this case. The major difference is that migrants from the district seat have often had a specific occupational trajectory in mind when they left and have often had substantial experience in the telegraph or postal services, or bureaucratic or administrative services connected with the district seat's judicial functions.

Beginning around 1960, Mexico City became the premier point of destination for migrants from all three communities. They chose the capital because of the tremendous set of opportunities concentrated there—especially in employment and education—opportunities that were matched nowhere else in the nation. The actual extent of this mobility, however, was constrained by variables that were the direct result of the level of development in the communities and region of origin, especially in regard to the educational systems and the kinds of nonfarm occupations that were available.

The growing concentration of migrants from each of the three communities in the capital represented a new stage and dynamic: a pattern of chain migration evolved in which new migrants were facilitated by old. Chain migration and facilitation in Mexico City, based on the norm of paisanazgo, produced a set of characteristic features, including a period in the late 1950s and early 1960s when migrants from each community clustered in certain neighborhoods and kinds of jobs (if not actual job locations), and migrant social relations were marked by visiting and participation in leisure activities among paisanos. In addition, many migrants began to participate in informal paisano networks of reciprocity and mutual aid.

During the 1960s and 1970s, some migrants from each of the three communities began to organize formal migrant associations in Mexico City. Although each had similar goals—which revolved around support for or opposition to development projects back in the home village or in the region as a whole—each association took on its own form and emphasis. Villaltecos in Mexico City, for example, formed a number of migrant associations that were essentially support groups for political factions back in Villa Alta. Apparently, political leaders there did not run these groups directly, but urban associations actively supported the positions and campaigns of either the Calero or the Progressive political groups in the district seat.

Since Ralu'a is a well-developed community and has an active and dynamic political leadership, Ralu'ans in Mexico City have been asked to support the town only on an ad hoc basis. Because a village association is unnecessary under these circumstances, Ralu'an leaders in Mexico City tried to organize migrants from both Ralu'a and the surrounding villages in the Rincón into broader regional coalitions. One such group had a strong interest in rural development. The other was an extension of an urban union, and while the rhetoric of its leaders emphasized development issues back home, the actual functions of the association had more to do with urban politics than with regional development per se. Both organizations were run by outmigrants.

Lahoyan village development associations revolved around a schism between a charismatic migrant leader—the professor—and factions in both the village and Mexico City that opposed his vision, efforts, and leadership. Fighting between these groups was very intense and did not abate even after the professor was killed in a mysterious "accident."

These conditions provide the basis for an examination of the conditions under which paisanazgo and migrant associations are organized. Paisanazgo is fairly widely distributed among migrants that originate from rural peasant backgrounds, and I have identified some basic conditions that framed its appearance as a force in Mountain Zapotec migrant social organization, including chain migration, an expanding urban job market that required large numbers of semiskilled and skilled workers, and overall numbers of migrants.

While it is certainly not true in every known case, politicization is often a key factor in the formation of a migrant association among indigenous peasant migrants in Latin America, and one that shapes its form and focus.[1] For the Mountain Zapotec case studies described here, I have emphasized the role of the Mexican state. From the 1960s through the 1980s, the Mexican government offered rural communities money and technical advice to create a range of infrastructure and health-oriented services. In each of the cases I have described, the formation and evolution of Mountain Zapotec migrant associations must be seen in this larger context. Beyond this, the three cases indicate that a migrant community's response has much to do with political configurations linking the points of origin and destination.

Norms similar to paisanazgo have manifested themselves widely among rural–urban migrants. To cite one example from Mexico involving other than indigenous peasants, Rollwagen's research on mestizo *paleteros* (who sell flavored ice confections)—especially in regard to their recruitment of laborers from the central highlands to work in Mexico City on the basis of "home town" ties—is an outstanding example, even though such ties are framed in terms of vertically oriented patron–client relationships (see Rollwagen 1974). Similarly, situations in which ties to a home town or home region served as the basis for mutual aid and associations have been reported in such diverse settings as among Chinese in Ch'ing-dynasty cities (Armentrout Ma 1984), internal migrants in Egyptian, Nigerian, and Greek cities (Abu-Lughod 1961; Dike 1982; and Kenna 1983, respectively), African migrants throughout West Africa (Little 1970; Eades 1979), and a plethora of migrant groups in various points of destination overseas: Japanese and Filipino settlers in Hawaii (Embree 1939:406–7; Okamura 1982), Italians in the United States and Great

Britain (Alba 1985:30, 47–49; Palmer 1991), South Asians in Great Britain and elsewhere (Clarke et al. 1990), Greeks and other southern Europeans in Australia (Price 1963), and southern Europeans in northern Europe (Castles et al. 1984; Rex et al. 1987).[2]

What is actually shared in these cases has to do with the proverbial encounter between market economies and what Meillassoux (1981) calls the domestic community. Nonetheless, care is essential when comparing migrant regional associations even when the similarities among cases are striking. If nothing else, I hope I have shown that different origins, linkages, and dynamics indelibly mark the organization and trajectories of regional associations even though a casual synchronic analysis might suggest they are functionally equivalent.

PAISANAZGO AS CULTURAL CAPITAL

I have claimed from the beginning that paisanazgo can be seen as a kind of "cultural capital" that Mountain Zapotec migrants have actively created and deployed to meet certain challenges that they have faced both in Mexico City and back home in the sierra.

The chief theoretician of the concept of cultural capital, French sociologist Pierre Bourdieu, developed it to help explain how matters of taste (artistic or otherwise), style and manners (as linked to, and as a reflection of, class), and "ease" are used by the elite in contemporary French academic and occupational settings both to distinguish themselves and also to pass along privilege to their progeny (Bourdieu 1984, 1986). In conjunction with economic and "social" capital (i.e., resources that come from being able to mobilize one's affiliation with a given group; Bourdieu 1986:248–49), cultural capital thus becomes another important, if subtle, resource that facilitates the reproduction of the overall class structure.

Without seeking to exaggerate its overall significance with respect to Bourdieu's brilliant exposition, my fieldwork among the Mountain Zapotec indicates that groups from other classes besides the elite in contemporary societies can draw from collective resources that are deeply rooted in their socioeconomic conditions for purposes of distinction and reproduction.

The Rincón Mountain Zapotec are, like other indigenous peasant communities in southern Mexico, distinctive from *mestizos* in their communal sensibilities and cooperative traditions. As Pozas and Pozas (1977:54–56) indicate in their classic study of indigenous peoples within the class structure of modern Mexico, such values and norms are passed along to children via the socialization process in the context of their families. Not only are cooperative practices part of a worldview, the former lie at the very base of economic production and thus the survival of the larger community (Pozas and Pozas

1977:40, 56–57). The point is that even today in both rural and urban settings, the Mountain Zapotec *do* have a stronger communal orientation than other Mexicans. Zapotecs are brought up to regard their natal community and its members as having legitimate needs and interests that may, if the circumstances warrant, be as important as those of any individual. Practices of *tequio* and *gozona* exemplify this orientation in Mountain Zapotec communities, although clearly their use varies from setting to setting in the sierra.

The norm of paisanazgo in the urban setting thus has twin origins, and these origins are fully complementary.[3] On the one hand, its roots are rural because the majority of those who are involved in its creation come from rural areas in the hinterlands of Oaxaca. In this sense, many of the migrants' cultural expressions in the city are deeply influenced by value orientations (such as pueblismo) and social institutions of cooperation found throughout the farming communities of the Sierra Juárez. On the other hand, paisanazgo is also fundamentally *urban* in nature because it develops in response to urban social, cultural, and economic conditions. Further proof lies in the fact that no individuals or communities in the sierra refer to paisanazgo per se or cite it as a norm underlying mutual aid in the provinces. Instead, paisanazgo is an integral part of contemporary urban life for many indigenous peasant migrants in sites like Mexico City, and its creation, use, and evolution in the capital are channeled by urban dynamics and by the availability or lack of resources and opportunities.

In the final analysis, then, paisanazgo represents a creative dynamic that both expresses and demonstrates a capacity for social and cultural recomposition on the part of Mountain Zapotec migrants in the Mexico City setting. As such, paisanazgo constitutes a form of "embodied" cultural capital in that it entails "legitimate cultural attitudes, preferences, and behaviors [which (Bourdieu) calls practices] that are internalized during the socialization process" (Lamont and Lareau 1988:156).[4] The term *socialization process* in this context refers to the socialization that takes place in both the provincial setting and the urban setting of Mexico City. What is outstanding about the Mountain Zapotec migrants is that, after 1960, practices of chain migration, facilitation, and association were socializing agents in and of themselves, in the sense that out-migrants drew from each to assemble viable, meaningful lives in the capital. Through relationships of facilitation and association, new migrants had access to a variety of resources held by their kin and paisanos. In turn, once they had settled, many decided to join the larger migrant community and share their personal and/or family resources with it in a similar fashion.

The above should not be taken to imply, however, that paisanazgo as a norm is somehow set in stone. While further research certainly needs to be done on this matter, the case studies discussed here support Cancian's hypothesis that norms can be subject to rapid change (Cancian 1975:158). Two developments in the 1980s indicate how and why this is so.

One development can be identified among the Lahoyan migrants in Mexico City. If the norm of paisanazgo is set in a context in which actual social relations become manipulative, nonegalitarian, or conflict ridden, major contradictions arise. This is because, at an ideological level and by definition, the rhetorical use of paisanazgo revolves around and evokes egalitarian sentiments and cooperative practices. Given this ideal, migrants react negatively to situations in which paisanazgo is made to serve as a screen or cover—or as an imperative—that masks negative or exploitive social relations. As is most notable in the Lahoyan case, migrants may end up cutting their ties to the migrant community, the community of origin, or both, preferring to go their own way because the price of affiliation with the group has become too high.

Second, because the regional boundaries underlying paisanazgo are fluid, under the right conditions paisanazgo can lend itself to other kinds of regional and ethnic alliance than are entailed in coming from the same village. Both Pitt-Rivers and Foster (with respect to rural agricultural settings in Spain) and Kearney (with respect to Mountain Zapotecs from the town of Ixtepeji) note that attitudes epitomized by pueblismo belie the fact that locals recognize affiliations and ties beyond the immediate community. Kearney's observation that Mountain Zapotecs from Ixtepeji think that their village is safer than neighboring communities but also think that the communities in the sierra are safer than those in the valley (Kearney 1972:24–26) is reminiscent of what anthropologists call the principle of "complementary opposition" within a segmentary lineage model: when faced by a common external threat, two or more lineages that have had strained relations or even out-and-out conflicts can suddenly reaffirm genealogical ties and be transformed into allies.

This point is important because it helps to account for two somewhat surprising developments in the sierra since the late 1970s: the formation of regional assemblies (Parnell 1988:82–85) and regional cooperatives whose aim is to achieve local control over the processes of economic development involving communal lands (Martínez Luna 1982; Bray 1991). Both developments naturally entail commitments above and beyond those represented by one's immediate community of origin. Alliances beyond the village level, however, have become imperative insofar as serranos, in order to defend their rights and autonomy, have decided to resist the intrusions of large businesses and even the state, as well as to combat the growing presence of Protestant messianic movements in the highlands of Oaxaca.

These recent trends underscore the fact that pueblismo, paisanazgo, and migrant village associations have all been energized and shaped by larger structural contexts and dynamics, such as the government's continuing projects of centralization, rural development, and the assimilation of indigenous peoples. Similarly, recent phenomena like the organization of regional assemblies, regional cooperatives, and regional-level migrant associations encompassing out-migrants from Oaxaca in California (see Nagengast and Kearney 1990, and Zabin 1992) represent the continuing responses of indigenous peasants who are trying collectively to control or address changes resulting from larger development processes that impact themselves, their families, and their communities. Evolving definitions of the region and regional commitments are thus part of the mix that will continue to unite and divide the residents and communities of the sierra, as well as their out-migrants, in new and unexpected ways.

REFERENCE MATERIAL

NOTES

CHAPTER 1. INTRODUCTION

1. As a norm, *paisanazgo* pertains to the domain of culture. In this sense, its evolution in the urban context and its innovative application to conditions there allow it to be seen as a kind of capital. (I owe thanks to two of the anonymous reviewers of my manuscript for independently suggesting this point; personal communications, 1991 and 1992.) Readers are cautioned from the beginning, however, that my use of the term *cultural capital* draws selectively from the larger theoretical project proposed by Bourdieu (Bourdieu and Wacquant 1992).

2. Nader 1969 and Whitecotton 1977 provide overviews of the Zapotec of Oaxaca; pertinent information can also be found in Nolasco 1972 and Romero Frizzi 1988. Ethnographies of specific Zapotec communities include Chiñas 1973 and Royce 1975 on the isthmus setting; de la Fuente [1949] 1977; Nader 1964; Kearney 1972; Berg 1974, 1976; and Parnell 1988 on the sierra, and Leslie 1960, Iszaevich 1973, Selby 1974, Dennis 1987, and Stephen 1991 on the valley.

3. Ralu'a, the marketing center I studied, and Lahoya, a nearby agricultural community, are both situated in the Rincón, a small area near the town of Villa Alta. Although it has no official status, the Rincón is recognized by its inhabitants as a distinct area east of the Río del Rincón and west of the Río Cajonos. In addition, members of the communities of the Rincón speak Nexitzo, one of the many languages that constitute Zapotec, and share a similar culture and environmental setting. Because I had extensive contact with Rincón Zapotec migrants, the bulk of my research focuses on them. I refer to all three communities as Mountain Zapotec because Villa Alta does not pertain to the Rincón. What is more, many of the Zapotec speakers in villages that belong to the larger municipality of Villa Alta speak Cajonos, not Nexitzo.

4. I have adapted the definition of *reciprocity network* proposed by Lomnitz, who defines it as a network in which "each participant exchanges goods and services with all other participants" (1977:132, 134–35; also see Vélez-Ibañez 1988).

5. Because important materials are available about Villalteco associations in both rural and urban settings, I chose to draw from secondary materials in order to compare and contrast them briefly with the communities that I studied firsthand. Fortunately, there is enough information in Parnell's 1988 study to provide a preliminary analysis of and response to these questions even while acknowledging that more extensive investigation will be necessary to elucidate the finer points.

6. Oliveira and Stern (1974) provide a clear presentation of the historical structural approach, contrasting it sharply with the modernization approach to migration studies.

7. I would like to acknowledge the influence of Professor Susan Buck Sutton, whose research on the relationship between the government's regional development programs and migrant associations in Greece attuned me to this process among the Zapotec (see Sutton 1978, 1983).

CHAPTER 2. PAISANAZGO AND MIGRANT ASSOCIATIONS

1. Another gloss of the term *paisano* refers to *campesino, habitante del campo,* (that is, a peasant), almost as if this were the kind of person who would be most likely to feel such sentiments (*Diccionario de la lengua española,* 2:994, [Madrid: Real Academia Española, 1984]).

2. Homans contrasts a "norm" with an "ideal," specifying that a norm is usually sanctioned, but an ideal reflects an ethical or moral principle or stand and does not generate either punishment or reward, at least in terms of the response of associates (Homans 1950:124). Values, on the other hand, are not explicitly formulated in terms of everyday life, and while they can be deduced from repeated "behavior and in casual remarks," they cannot necessarily be articulated by the person or group holding them (Homans 1950:127–28). Homans, following Kluckhohn and Kelly, specifies that culture is "a historically derived system of explicit and implicit designs for living, which tends to be shared by all or specifically designated members of a group" (Homans 1950:125). On this basis, Homans argues that while norms are a part of culture, they are not its direct equivalent because culture involves both ideas and behavior; norms are "statements of what ought to be, and only this" (Homans 1950:125). While I agree with this view of culture, below I contest Homans's overall view of norms.

3. See Foster 1960:36–37 for illustrations of *dichos* in Spain: "ubiquitous rhymes and sayings which eulogize the qualities the sons of a pueblo believe should make it the envy of the world and which ridicule all other places." To my knowledge, such dichos did not develop among Ralu'ans or Lahoyans in either the sierra or Mexico City.

4. The definition and meaning of *ethnicity* in Latin America have been the subject of a voluminous literature. Regarding Middle America, I have found useful overviews in Borah 1954; de la Fuente 1967; CLALI 1983; Díaz Polanco 1984, 1987; and Bonfil Batalla 1987, 1988. As Adams (1989) points out, though, a plethora of approaches has been offered in the literature over the years. For heuristic purposes, in Mexico these can be classified as highlighting ethnocultural (e.g., Gamio 1942), ethnoterritorial (e.g., Aguirre Beltrán 1979), or class (e.g., Díaz Polanco 1984; Arizpe 1988) dimensions, or some combination of the above, often in terms of a model based on an "internal colonial" perspective (e.g., González Casanova 1970:84–103; Stavenhagen 1986a, 1986b, 1989).

5. It is worth noting here that only toward the end of my stay (and also in reflecting upon my experiences in the field once I returned home) did I begin to fully realize the extent to which Ralu'ans *chose* to emphasize their unity and solidarity as paisanos in Mexico City. Although not all interviews or data support this image, I

have highlighted these characteristics in my ethnographic descriptions, partly because I believe this is what the Ralu'ans intended for me to perceive and convey. The analytical status of the concept of paisanazgo, then, is both "emic" and "etic"; it is at once a concept and a norm employed by the Ralu'an migrants and an analytic device that I use to describe and analyze Mountain Zapotec migrant culture and social organization. At the same time, as will become evident in the analysis and conclusion, I have subjected the norm of paisanazgo to critical scrutiny, especially in considering its deployment insofar as it has contributed to intragroup division among Mountain Zapotec migrants.

6. By "non-statutory" Pickvance means "not established by law."

7. I have drawn from Mangin 1959, Doughty 1976, and especially Altamirano 1984a in formulating this definition of migrant associations.

8. It is important to emphasize, however, that regional associations serve few if any unique functions. That is, an examination of urban studies carried out throughout Latin America demonstrates that virtually all functions described below are carried out by groups other than those based on common origin.

9. Prof. Ben Kobashigawa of San Francisco State University, a specialist on Okinawans in the United States, suggested the hypothesis that, all things being equal, migrants try to form associations in terms of the most immediate territorial base within a given region, since primary group relationships are more pervasive there (personal communication, 1985).

10. To be fair, Bataillon also acknowledges that other kinds of social ties can underlie mutual aid patterns among out-migrants who cluster in certain occupations in Mexico City. He notes that some workers help each other out because they come from the same state (in his case, Oaxaca).

11. Interested readers should also note that Orellana S. 1973 discusses the close parallel between the political organization of the municipality of Soyaltepec and the organization of the migrant associations formed by Mixtec migrants from Soyaltepec in Mexico City.

12. Laite and Long (1987) provide a recent application of this same perspective, treating ethnographic data concerning the *corta monte* (tree-cutting) ceremony in selected highland communities of Peru.

13. Readers should remember that many informal relationships are based on "common origin." Butterworth's studies of migrants from Tilantongo in Mexico City (e.g., 1970, 1972; see also Butterworth and Chance 1981), and Altamirano's research on Quechua and Aymara migrants in Lima (e.g., 1984a, 1988), document a full range of such relationships.

CHAPTER 3. THE RURAL–URBAN INTERFACE

1. These efforts included the establishment of INI centers in both the Sierra Juárez and the Mixe areas of Oaxaca during the 1950s.

2. Corbett and Whiteford's analysis (1983) provides a useful basis for understanding the impact of modernization and state penetration on the indigenous peasant communities of Oaxaca. The authors distinguish between ideological, institutional, and structural levels of government penetration, and discuss separately the extension

of services, infrastructure, organizations, and political parties within the structural level.

3. A fascinating autobiography by Lini De Vries (1972) provides a firsthand account of a Papaloapan Commission health worker's experiences in the Mixe area and the Sierra Zapoteca, among other locales. It is interesting to juxtapose De Vries's reminiscences of the terrible health conditions that she and many others worked so hard to ameliorate with Boege's wholesale condemnation of the commission's activities in the Mazatec area (see Boege 1988). My own sense is that the commission's work in Oaxaca was varied in its intensity and impact.

4. Varese's research on the impact of national education on Zapotec Indians and his subsequent attempts to find ways to reverse the resulting cultural damage (1983, 1985) provide a thought-provoking review of this topic.

5. My understanding of Mexico City as an urban context within the larger nation derives primarily from two outstanding accounts by teams of Mexican social scientists: Unikel et al. (1976) and the collective and individual work of sociologists Humberto Muñoz, Orlandina de Oliveira, and Claudio Stern (e.g., Muñoz, Oliveira, and Stern 1977; Oliveira 1976; Stern 1982).

6. In this sense, Mexico City can be properly characterized as a primate city (see the formula presented by Unikel [1971]). Insofar as the bureaucrats of the primate city control the government and economy of the nation, a primate city is the center of the nation's development and growth, dominating other cities as well as the hinterlands (Fox 1977; Armstrong and McGee 1985).

7. For earlier writings on the process of fieldwork, see Lewis 1953 and Williams 1967 and the overviews by Nader (1977) and Junker (1960), the latter of which is set within the framework of the Chicago school of urban sociology. To mention only a few examples of the technical literature on setting up and doing fieldwork, there are the contributions of Brim and Spain (1974), the Peltos (1978), and Bernard (1988) on the construction of research designs and fieldwork methods, as well as an interesting anthology on fieldnotes edited by Sanjek (1990).

8. Stimulating presentations of anthropological perspectives on urban settings are available in Fox 1977 and Hannerz 1980. A recent volume by Mitchell (1987) introduces a wide range of specific conceptual and methodological issues in urban anthropology, which are resolved vis-à-vis Mitchell's extensive fieldwork data from Africa. In addition, Kearney's overview (1986) is an excellent survey of how current debates in political economy and interpretive anthropology have influenced the ethnographic approach in migration and development studies.

9. Myrdal (1969) and González Casanova (1981) provide examples of two social scientists (an economist and a sociologist) who are committed to the position that explicit methodological discussions are key to objectivity in the social sciences. The study by González Casanova is important for its examination of the epistemology of the social sciences and its proposal that the researcher's most fundamental assumptions can and should be explicitly revealed and put to the test.

10. An important preliminary step I carried out that summer was to explain the focus of my research, in writing, to the municipal authorities and to request their permission to carry out research in Ralu'a. This insured that I had formally and publicly registered with local officials my presence as an anthropologist and my intention to study the topic of out-migration (see note 12, below).

11. This questionnaire was originally developed for a study of the *favelas* (squatter settlements) of Rio, many of whose inhabitants were also migrants; see Perlman (1974, 1976). I adapted a Spanish translation of this questionnaire, almost in its entirety, for the reasons given in the text.

12. Unlike in the Mountain Zapotec communities of origin, there was no central authority among the out-migrants in Mexico City that I could go to in order to explain my research topic and request formal permission to do my research. I handled this, first, by affiliating with a Mexican university, the Colegio de México, and keeping in contact with professors in the Centro de Estudios Sociológicos regarding the evolving focus of my research. Second, among Zapotec migrants themselves, I did my interviews on the basis of informed consent. The American Anthropological Association has issued a number of formal guidelines that are useful to study before and while engaging in fieldwork. One example is the "Principles of Professional Responsibility" (AAA 1989), which discusses ethical priorities and places them into the larger context of the competing sets of interests that an anthropologist is likely to face in a field situation.

13. Because my Ralu'an sample was nonrandom and because I found that official Mexican census data on Ralu'a itself were at best estimates, quantitative materials throughout the text should be taken only as approximations. Also, at no point in any of the interviews were the people I interviewed paid for their cooperation, partly because many of them were either relatives, *padrinos* (ritual godparents), or good friends of my Ralu'an host families in the town and in Mexico City. Later I also found out that, since I was doing a study on migrants from Ralu'a and approached Ralu'ans as a U.S. student interested in learning about Mexico and the Zapotec, people were ready to cooperate gratis.

14. Essentially, employment in the formal sector of the economy implies a job that (1) is attached to the urban industrial process of production, (2) is stable, (3) provides a steady income, and (4) allows access to urban services (Lomnitz 1977:9–14). Thus, employment in the formal sector has a critical impact on the stability of household income and standard of living generally.

CHAPTER 4. THE COMMUNITIES OF ORIGIN

1. See Chance 1989 for the most extensive treatment of the Sierra Zapoteca, including the area that is now the district of Villa Alta, during the colonial period.

2. The term *self-provisioning* (employed by Kate Young [1982]) rather than *self-sufficient* is used throughout the text to emphasize that, to one degree or another, the peasants of the Sierra Juárez are integrated into regional, state, and national marketing systems as both producers and consumers (Beals 1971, 1975, 1979).

3. It must be remembered that high rates of out-migration during the 1960s and 1970s effectively eliminated population pressures on arable land in Lahoya, and by the middle of the 1970s many of the fields that were some distance from the village were simply no longer being cultivated.

4. Nader's research indicates that the practice of *tequio* and other forms of mutual aid vary from village to village in the sierra, both in frequency and usage (1964; also see Beals 1971).

5. The 1950 census is used here for two reasons. First, it presents the most detailed information available from the national census on civil status and household size and composition. Second, the data also effectively capture the background from whence most of the out-migrants from Lahoya in Mexico City came.

6. My own data, along with subsequent reports on religion in the sierra offered by Marroquín (1987, 1989), indicate that Protestant evangelists have made little headway in this particular village.

7. *Aguardiente* and *mescal* are the most common alcoholic drinks produced and consumed in the village. Drinking is a common pastime, and although women abstained formerly, in recent years it has been reported that some now drink almost as much as the men.

8. The prevalence of witchcraft in a given social setting has been correlated with a decentralized authority system; see the ethnographic account presented in *Paiute Sorcery* (Whiting 1950) (Nader, personal communication).

9. A Lahoyan friend once commented, as he was playing a tape recording of the different styles of music from Lahoya—*danzón, fantasía, bolero,* and "*música de allá*"—that the pieces might not sound so great compared to a recording of professional musicians. I was told, though, that one had to understand that, as full-time farmers, Lahoyans play music only as a part-time cultural activity. It is only in this context, my friend emphasized, that one could really appreciate what the musicianship of the villagers really represents.

10. To my knowledge, no one has studied the economics of coffee production in Ralu'a in any depth. Excellent background studies, which can be consulted for an understanding of the coffee market in Oaxaca in general can be found in Downing 1980 and Nolasco 1985.

11. My thanks to Dr. Kate Young and her associates for sharing a prepublication version of this census with me. She subsequently referred to it in one of her publications (Young 1978a:144).

12. Clearly, this situation has not always been the case. Ralu'a had periods when work was scarce, labor was plentiful, and day wages were very low. Life histories, as well as studies of economic trends within the region as a whole (Berg 1974; Young 1978a), indicate that two periods were especially difficult for wage laborers: the mid-1930s and again when the price of coffee fell in the late 1950s.

13. For further details on this custom, which is actually quite widely practiced throughout Mexico, see Nader 1964 and Pozas and Pozas 1977. Some specialists in the pre-Hispanic and colonial periods believe that mutual aid practices like *gozona* had both indigenous and European roots (see, e.g., Borah 1976).

14. Some of the bilingual residents of Ralu'a, for example, made a special point of telling me how enjoyable it was to speak Zapotec on a day-to-day basis out in the fields or on social occasions when one's rhetorical skills could be displayed or a sense of humor was called for.

15. Ignacio Reyes Ruiz, a Zapotec schoolteacher who was not born in the region but who worked there, has offered a rather harsh portrait of the Villaltecos as mestizo exploiters preying on the Zapotec peasants from the surrounding villages (Reyes Ruiz 1981). While there is, no doubt, an element of truth to his charges, Reyes's denial that the Villaltecos are oriented toward *any* of the local forms of mutual aid casts some suspicion on the overall accuracy, if not the objectivity, of his account.

CHAPTER 5. PATTERNS OF OUT-MIGRATION

1. The presentation on Lahoya is much more tentative and generalized than the presentation on Ralu'a. This is because of the small sample size and the difficulty in verifying all of the information obtained.

2. Transportation became somewhat improved with the building of roads into the sierra, such as the road that linked the important mining center of Natividad to Oaxaca City (Pérez García 1956, 2:292).

3. I was not able to collect many detailed case studies as examples because (1) their overall numbers were smaller, and (2) the many intervening years in the city, and contact with more recent migrants, has changed the early migrants' outlook (also, see note 6 below).

4. The latter families had two reactions. One was an awareness of the need to diversify, if only to grow larger amounts of subsistence or other cash crops besides coffee, and the other was a desire to send one or more children out of the village.

5. See Singer 1977:9 for an interesting analysis of this phenomenon, generally speaking.

6. I also found that many of the early migrants were upwardly mobile and had achieved a measure of security by the time that the second period of out-migration began twenty years later. The early migrants were influenced by the second group. Thus, in a brief conversation, early migrants might give aspirational motives for leaving the village; but in a more detailed discussion, stories about conditions in the village would always arise as major factors resulting in migration.

CHAPTER 6. REGIONAL BASES OF MIGRANT SOCIAL RELATIONS

1. Representatives from each of the two factions had differing perspectives on this basic situation. His detractors claimed that the professor was suspect because he arranged to have government funds for village development projects given to him directly. This arrangement was clearly outside of "proper channels," that is, the municipal authorities back in Lahoya. But the professor's supporters claimed that he was an upright citizen. Moreover, they say, his policy of receiving government funds directly was a perspicacious strategy because in one stroke he retained control and circumvented the elite families of the village.

2. Readers should note that this index hides the adaptation process of the two waves of migrants described previously because by the late 1970s economic and material differences had leveled out. In fact, it took the members of the first wave much more time and effort to achieve their positions because they had to operate essentially on their own.

3. In 1978 there were twenty-two pesos to the dollar.

4. In fact, all but a few homes I observed were in far better condition than those in the inner city or in the peripheral neighborhoods around Mexico City (as compared to the housing described in Lomnitz 1977:18–19, 78–81).

5. Telephone service was difficult and expensive to obtain during this period.

6. A Ralu'an migrant activist who participated in this organization reported that

the factional division between the Lahoyans was carried into, and greatly disrupted, some of the Regional Zapotec Association's meetings in Mexico City.

CHAPTER 7. ETHNOGRAPHIC ANALYSIS

1. For a sophisticated discussion of how local classes and class dynamics can impact visions of regional culture, see Lomnitz-Adler 1991.
2. Claude Fischer (1976) presents a very useful overview of how "critical mass" affects urban ethnic communities, although he mentions no precise figure at which this variable becomes salient. Rose Hum Lee once observed that for an urban Chinatown to evolve, some 250 persons were needed (Lee 1949:424–25).
3. It remains to be seen, however, whether the other indigenous Oaxacan populations who have out-migrants in Mexico City have organized or will organize themselves in a similar fashion. In 1980 these groups included, for example, some 3,762 Mazatecs, 1,343 Chinantecs, 221 Chontals, 175 Cuicatecs, and 80 Chatinos (Barabas y Bartolomé 1986:73).
4. I have found De la Peña's (1986) discussion of power in local contexts in Mexico very useful for this analysis.

CHAPTER 8. CONCLUSION

1. This is not the whole answer to the question, of course. For extended comparative examinations of how and why migrant associations form in Latin American cities, see Altamirano 1984a and Hirabayashi 1986.
2. For a more extensive listing and discussion of comparative materials pertaining to regional ties among migrants from the provinces in urban settings, see Altamirano and Hirabayashi forthcoming.
3. I owe thanks to Professor Teófilo Altamirano, of the Catholic University of Peru, for bringing this point to my attention.
4. Bourdieu's writings suggest that practices pertaining to the *implementation* of relationships based on paisanazgo fall within the domain of "social capital" (Bourdieu 1986:248–52, 256n.12; Bourdieu and Wacquant 1992:118–20). By contrast, my discussion of paisanazgo as an embodied form of cultural capital emphasizes (1) its historical roots in a provincial communal setting; (2) its creative genesis in response to the challenges of life in the urban setting; and (3) its formal transmission through a process of socialization. In this regard, socialization in either the provinces or the city is not a casual or random process; it involves "personal cost" in terms of the "privation, renunciation, and sacrifice" that both the inculcation and practice of communally oriented norms entail (Bourdieu 1986:244). In its roots, genesis, and ensocialized qualities, then, paisanazgo seems to go well beyond "social capital" and in the final analysis represents "external wealth converted into an integral part of the person" (Bourdieu 1986:244–45).

BIBLIOGRAPHY

Abu-Lughod, Janet. 1961. "Migrant Adjustment to City Life: The Egyptian Case." *American Journal of Sociology* 47:22-32.
Adams, Richard N. 1967. "Nationalization." In Manning Nash, ed., *Handbook of Middle American Indians*, 6:469-89. Austin: University of Texas Press.
———. 1989. "Internal and External Ethnicities: With Special Reference to Central America." In Asociación Centroamericana de Sociología (ACAS), *Estado, Democratización y Desarrollo en Centroamerica y Panama*, 475-99. Guatemala City: ACAS.
Aguierre Beltrán, Gonzalo. 1979. *Regions of Refuge*. Washington, D.C.: Society for Applied Anthropology.
Alba, Richard D. 1985. *Italian Americans: Into the Twilight of Ethnicity*. Englewood Cliffs, N.J.: Prentice-Hall.
Alexander, June Granatir. 1981. "Staying Together: Chain Migration and Patterns of Slovak Settlement in Pittsburgh Prior to World War I." *Journal of American Ethnic History* 1:56-83.
Altamirano, Teófilo. 1984a. *Presencia andina en Lima metropolitana: Un estudio sobre migrantes y clubes de provincianos*. Lima: Pontificia Universidad Católica del Perú.
———. 1984b. "Regional Commitment Among Central Highlands Migrants in Lima." In Norman Long and Bryan Roberts, eds., *Miners, Peasants and Entrepreneurs: Regional Development in the Central Highlands of Peru*, 198-215. New York: Cambridge University Press.
———. 1988. *Cultura andina y pobreza urbana: Aymaras en Lima metropolitana*. Lima: Pontificia Universidad Católica del Perú.
Altamirano, Teófilo, and Lane Ryo Hirabayashi, eds. Forthcoming. *Migrants, Regional Cultures, and Latin American Cities*. Society for Latin American Anthropology Publication Series. Washington, D.C.: American Anthropological Association.
American Anthropological Association. 1989. "Proposed Draft Revision of the Principles of Professional Responsibility," *Anthropology Newsletter*, 30:22-23.
Arizpe S., Lourdes. 1975. *Indígenas en la ciudad de México: El caso de las 'Marias.'* SepSetentas series, no. 182. Mexico City: Secretaría de Educación Pública.
———. 1978. *Migración, etnicismo y cambio económico: Un estudio sobre migrantes campesinos a la ciudad de México*. Mexico City: El Colegio de México.

———. 1988. "Anthropology in Latin America: Old Boundaries, New Contexts." In Christopher Mitchell, ed., *Changing Perspectives in Latin American Studies: Insights From Six Disciplines*, 143–61. Stanford, Calif.: Stanford University Press.

Armentrout Ma., L. Eve. 1984. "Fellow-Regional Associations in the Ch'ing Dynasty: Organizations in Flux for Mobile People; A Preliminary Survey." *Modern Asian Studies* 18:307–30.

Armstrong, Warwick, and T. G. McGee. 1985. *Theatres of Accumulation: Studies in Asian and Latin American Urbanization*. New York: Methuen.

Avellaneda Díaz, Ximena. 1990. "Los Grupos Étnicos del Estado de Oaxaca." *América Indígena* 2/3:342–63.

Barabas, Alicia M., and Miguel A. Bartolomé, eds. 1986. *Etnicidad y pluralismo cultural: La dinámica étnica en Oaxaca*. Mexico City: Instituto Nacional de Antropología e Historia.

Basañez E., Miguel, ed. 1987. *La composición del poder: Oaxaca, 1968–1984*. Mexico City: Instituto Nacional de Administración Pública.

Bataillon, Claude. 1972. *La ciudad y el campo en el México central*. Mexico City: Siglo Veintiuno.

Beals, Ralph L. 1967. "Acculturation." In Manning Nash, ed., *Handbook of Middle American Indians*, 6:449–68. Austin: University of Texas Press.

———. 1971. "Estudio de poblados en la Sierra Zapoteca de Oaxaca, México." *América Indígena* 31:671–91.

———. 1975. *The Peasant Marketing System of Oaxaca, Mexico*. Berkeley: University of California Press.

———. 1979. "Some Social and Economic Implications of an Open Peasant Marketing System." In Aubrey Williams, ed., *Social, Political, and Economic Life in Contemporary Oaxaca*, 23–42. Vanderbilt Publications in Anthropology, No. 24. Nashville, Tenn.: Vanderbilt University.

Berg, Richard Lewis, Jr. 1974. *El impacto de la economía moderna: Sobre la economía tradicional de Zoogocho, Oaxaca y su area circundante*. Mexico City: Instituto Nacional Indigenista y Secretaría de Educación Pública.

———. 1976. *Shwan: A Highland Zapotec Woman*. New York: Vantage Press.

Bernard, H. Russell. 1988. *Research Methods in Cultural Anthropology*. Newbury Park, Calif.: Sage Press.

Boege, Eckart. 1988. *Los Mazatecos ante la nación: Contradicciones de la identidad étnica en México actual*. Mexico City: Siglo Veintiuno Editores.

Bonfil Batalla, Guillermo. 1987. "Los pueblos indios: Sus culturas y la políticas culturales." In Néstor García Canclini, ed., *Políticas culturales en América Latina*, 89–125. Mexico City: Grijalbo.

———. 1988. "La teoría del control cultural en el estudio de procesos étnicos." *Anuario Antropológico* 86:13–53.

Borah, Woodrow. 1954. "Race and Class in Mexico." *Pacific Historical Review* 23:331–42.

———. 1976. "Legacies of the Past: Colonial." In James W. Wilkie, M. C. Meyer, and E. Monzón de Wilkie, eds. *Contemporary Mexico*, 29–37. Berkeley: University of California Press, and the Colegio de México.

Bourdieu, Pierre. 1977. *Outline of a Theory of Practice*. New York: Cambridge University Press.

———. 1984. *Distinction: A Social Critique of the Judgment of Taste*. Cambridge, Mass.: Harvard University Press.

———. 1986. "The Forms of Capital." In John G. Richardson, ed., *Handbook of Theory and Research for the Sociology of Education*, 241–58. New York: Greenwood Press.

Bourdieu, Pierre, and Loïc J. D. Wacquant. 1992. *An Invitation to Reflexive Sociology*. Chicago: University of Chicago Press.

Bray, David Barton. 1991. "The Struggle for the Forest: Conservation and Development in the Sierra Juárez." *Grassroots Development* 15:13–25.

Brim, John A., and David H. Spain. 1974. *Research Design in Anthropology: Paradigms and Pragmatics in the Testing of Hypotheses*. New York: Holt, Rinehart and Winston.

Butterworth, Douglas. 1962. "A Study of the Urbanization Process Among Mixtec Migrants from Tilantongo in Mexico City." *América Indígena* 22:257–74.

———. 1970. "From Royalty to Poverty: The Decline of a Rural Mexican Community." *Human Organization* 29:5–11.

———. 1972. "Two Small Groups: A Comparison of Migrants and Non-Migrants in Mexico City." *Urban Anthropology* 1:29–50.

———. 1975. *Tilantongo: Comunidad mixteca en transción*. Mexico City: Instituto Nacional Indigenista.

Butterworth, Douglas, and John K. Chance. 1981. *Latin American Urbanization*. New York: Cambridge University Press.

Cabrera Acevedo, Gustavo. 1975. "Migración y actividad económica en México, 1960–1970." *Cahiers des Ameriques Latines*, Sciences de l'Homme ser., 12:3–31.

Campbell, Howard. 1990. "The COCEI: Culture, Class, and Politicized Ethnicity in the Isthmus of Tehuantepec." *Ethnic Groups* 8:29–56.

Cancian, Francesca M. 1975. *What Are Norms? A Study of Beliefs and Action in a Maya Community*. New York: Cambridge University Press.

Castles, Stephen, Heather Booth, and Tina Wallace. 1984. *Here for Good: Western Europe's New Ethnic Minorities*. London: Pluto Press.

Cederström, Thoric. 1989. Migrant Village Associations and Community Development in the Mixteca Region of Mexico. Paper presented at the annual meetings of the American Anthropological Association, Washington D.C., November 15, 1989.

———. 1990. "Migrant Remittances and Agricultural Development." *Culture and Agriculture* (Bulletin of the Cultural and Agriculture Group, American Anthropological Association) 40 (Fall/Winter): 2–7.

Chance, John K. 1971. "Kinship and Urban Residence: Household and Family Organization in a Suburb of Oaxaca, Mexico." *Journal of the Steward Anthropological Society* 2:122–47.

———. 1989. *Conquest of the Sierra: Spaniards and Indians in Colonial Oaxaca*. Norman: University of Oklahoma Press.

Chiñas, Beverly. 1973. *The Isthmus Zapotecs: Women's Roles in Cultural Context*. New York: Holt, Rinehart and Winston.

Clarke, Colin, Ceri Peach, and Steven Vertovec, eds. 1990. *South Asians Overseas: Migration and Ethnicity*. New York: Cambridge University Press.

Cohen, Abner. 1969. *Custom and Politics in Urban Africa: A Study of Hausa Migrants in Yoruba Towns*. Berkeley: University of California Press.

Consejo Latinoamericano de Apoyo a las Luchas Indígenas (CLALI). 1983. "Sobre la cuestión étnico-nacional en América Latina." *Boletín de Antropología Americana* 7:41–47.

Corbett, Jack, and Scott Whiteford. 1983. "State Penetration and Development in Mesoamerica, 1950–1980." In Carl Kendall, John Hawkins, and Laurel Bossen, eds., *Heritage of Conquest: Thirty Years Later,* 9–33. Albuquerque: University of New Mexico Press.

Covarrubias, Miguel. 1946. *Mexico South: The Isthmus of Tehuantepec.* New York: Knopf.

De la Fuente, Julio. [1949] 1977. *Yalalag: Una villa zapoteca serrana.* Mexico City: Instituto Nacional Indigenista.

———. 1965. *Relaciones interétnicas.* Mexico City: Instituto Nacional Indigenista.

———. 1967. "Ethnic Relationships." In Manning Nash, ed., *Handbook of Middle American Indians,* 6:432–48. Austin: University of Texas Press.

De la Peña, Guillermo. 1986. "Poder local, poder regional: Perspectivas socio-antropológicas." In Jorge N. Padua and Alain Venneph, eds., *Poder Local, Poder Regional,* 27–56. Mexico City: El Colegio de México.

Dennis, Philip A. 1976. *Conflictos por tierras en el valle de Oaxaca.* Mexico City: Instituto Nacional Indigenista.

———. 1987. *Intervillage Conflict in Oaxaca.* New Brunswick, N.J.: Rutgers University Press.

Depres, Leo A., ed. 1975. *Ethnicity and Resource Competition in Plural Societies.* The Hague: Mouton.

De Vries, Lini M. 1972. *Please, God, Take Care of the Mule.* Mexico City: Minutiae Mexicana.

Díaz Polanco, Héctor. 1984. "Notas teórico-metodológicas para el estudio de la cuestión étnica." *Boletín de Antropología Americana* 10:45–51.

———. 1987. "Lo nacional y lo étnico en México: El misterio de los projectos." Chapter 2 in *Etnia, Nación y Política,* 41–65. Mexico City: Juan Pablos Editor.

Dike, Azuka A. 1982. "Urban Migrants and Rural Development." *African Studies Review* 25:85–94.

Dirección General de Estadística. 1936. *Quinto censo general de población—1930.* Estado de Oaxaca vol. Mexico City.

———. 1946. *Sexto censo general de población—1940.* Estado de Oaxaca vol. Mexico City.

———. 1954. *Séptimo censo general de población—1950.* Estado de Oaxaca. Mexico City.

———. 1963. *Octavo censo general de población—1960.* Estado de Oaxaca. Mexico City.

———. 1973. *Noveno censo general de población—1970.* Estado de Oaxaca. Mexico City.

Doughty, Paul L. 1976. "The Social Lives of Migrants: The Case of Provincial Voluntary Associations in Lima." *Actes du XLII Congrés International des Américanistes* (Paris) 10:331–37.

———. 1979. "A Latin American Specialty in the World Context: Urban Primacy." *Urban Anthropology* 8:383–98.

Downing, Teodoro. 1980. "La penetración de los sectores privado y público en las zonas cafetaleras de México." In Iván Restrepo, ed., *Conflicto entre ciudad y campo en América Latina*, 275–311. Mexico City: Editorial Nueva Imagin.
Dunbar Ortiz, Roxanne. 1984. *Indians of the Americas: Human Rights and Self-Determination*. New York: Praeger.
Eades, J. S. 1979. "Kinship and Entrepreneurship Among Yoruba in Northern Ghana." In William A. Shack and Elliot P. Skinner, eds., *Changing Social Structure in Ghana*, 37–57. London: International African Institute.
Eckholm, Erik P. 1977. "The Deterioration of Mountain Environments." *Science* 189:764–70.
Embree, John F. 1939. "New and Local Kin Groups Among the Japanese Farmers of Kona, Hawaii." *American Anthropologist* 41:400–407.
Ewald, Robert H. 1967. "Directed Change." In Manning Nash, ed., *Handbook of Middle American Indians*, 6:490–511. Austin: University of Texas Press.
Fischer, Claude S. 1976. *The Urban Experience*. New York: Harcourt Brace Jovanovich.
Foster, George M. 1960. *Culture and Conquest: America's Spanish Heritage*. Viking Fund Pulications in Anthropology, No. 27. New York: Wenner-Gren Foundation for Anthropological Research.
Fox, Richard G. 1977. *Urban Anthropology: Cities in Their Cultural Settings*. Englewood Cliffs, N.J.: Prentice-Hall.
Gamio, Manuel. 1942. "Las características culturales y los censos indígenas." *América Indígena* 2:15–19.
Goering, John M. 1989. "Introduction and Overview." *International Migration Review* 23:797–812. Special issue: *The 'Explosiveness' of Chain Migration: Research and Policy Issues*.
Golte, Jürgen, and Norma Adams. 1987. *Los caballos de Troya de los invasores: Estrategias campesinas en la conquista de la gran Lima*. Lima: Instituto de Estudios Peruanos.
Goode, Judith Granich. 1970. "Latin American Urbanism and Corporate Groups." *Anthropological Quarterly* 43:146–67.
González Casanova, Pablo. 1970. *Democracy in Mexico*. New York: Oxford University Press.
———. 1981. *The Fallacy of Social Science Research: A Critical Examination and New Qualitative Model*. New York: Pergamon Press.
Gordon, Milton M. 1964. *Assimilation in American Life*. New York: Oxford University Press.
Greenberg, James B. 1990. "Sanctity and Resistance in Closed Corporate Indigenous Communities: Coffee Money, Violence, and Ritual Organization in Chatino Communities in Oaxaca." In Lynn Stephen and James Dow, eds., *Class, Politics, and Popular Religion in Mexico and Central America*, 95–114. Society for Latin American Anthropology Publication Series, 10. Washington, D.C.: American Anthropological Association.
Hamnett, Brian R. 1971. *Politics and Trade in Southern Mexico, 1750–1821*. New York: Cambridge University Press.
Hannerz, Ulf. 1980. *Exploring the City: Inquiries Toward an Urban Anthropology*. New York: Columbia University Press.

Hirabayashi, Lane Ryo. 1983. "On the Formation of Associations in Mexico: Mixtec and Mountain Zapotec Cases." *Urban Anthropology* 12:29–44.

———. 1986. "The Migrant Village Association in Latin America: A Comparative Analysis." *Latin American Research Review* 21:7–29.

Homans, George C. 1950. *The Human Group*. New York: Harcourt, Brace and Company.

Hunt, Eva, and June Nash. 1967. "Local and Territorial Units." In Manning Nash, ed., *Handbook of Middle American Indians*, 6:253–82. Austin: University of Texas Press.

Instituto Nacional de Estadística Geografía e Informática. 1984. *Décimo censo general de población y vivienda, 1980*. Estado de Oaxaca. Vol. 20, pts. 1–2. Mexico City.

Iszaevich, Abraham. 1973. *Modernización en una comunidad oaxaqueña del valle*. SepSetentas series, no. 109. Mexico City: Secretaría de Educación Pública.

Jongkind, Fred. 1974. "A Reappraisal of the Role of Regional Associations of Lima, Peru." *Comparative Studies in Society and History* 16:471–82.

———. 1986. "Ethnic Solidarity and Social Stratification: Migrant Organizations in Peru and Argentina." *Boletín de Estudios Latinoamericanos y del Caribe* 40:37–48.

Junker, Buford H. 1960. *Field Work: An Introduction to the Social Sciences*. Chicago: University of Chicago Press.

Kearney, Michael. 1972. *The Winds of Ixtepeji: World View and Society in a Zapotec Town*. New York: Holt, Rinehart and Winston.

———. 1986. "From the Invisible Hand to Visible Feet: Anthropological Studies of Migration and Development." *Annual Review of Anthropology* 15:331–61.

Kemper, Robert Van. 1977. *Migration and Adaptation: Tzintzuntzan Peasants in Mexico City*. Beverly Hills: Sage.

———. 1988. "Migration and Adaptation: Tzintzuntzeños in Mexico City." In George Gmelch and Walter P. Zenner, eds., *Urban Life: Readings in Urban Anthropology*, 180–88. Prospect Heights, Ill.: Waveland Press.

Kenna, Margaret. 1983. "Institutional and Transformational Migration and the Politics of Community: Greek Internal Migrants and the Migrants' Associations in Athens." *Archives Européennes de Sociologie* 24:263–67.

Knight, Alan. 1990. "Racism, Revolution, and *Indigenismo*: Mexico, 1910–1940." In Richard Graham, ed., *The Idea of Race in Latin America, 1870–1940*, 71–114. Austin: University of Texas Press.

Laite, Julian, and Norman Long. 1987. "Fiestas and Uneven Capitalist Development in Central Peru." *Bulletin of Latin American Research* 6:27–53.

Lamont, Michèle, and Annette Lareau. 1988. "Cultural Capital: Allusions, Gaps and Glissandos in Recent Theoretical Developments." *Sociological Theory* 6:153–68.

Lee, Rose Hum. 1949. "The Decline of Chinatowns in the United States." *American Journal of Sociology* 54:422–32.

Leslie, Charles. 1960. *Now We Are Civilized: A Study of the World View of the Zapotec Indians of Mitla, Oaxaca*. Detroit: Wayne State University Press.

Lewis, Oscar. 1952. "Urbanization Without Breakdown." *Scientific Monthly* 75:31–41.

———. 1953. "Controls and Experiments in Field Work." *Anthropology Today*, ed. A. L. Kroeber, 452–75. Chicago: University of Chicago Press.
Little, Kenneth. 1970. *West African Urbanization: A Study of Voluntary Associations in Social Change*. London: Cambridge University Press.
Lomnitz, Larissa Adler. 1977. *Networks and Marginality: Life in a Mexican Shantytown*. New York: Academic Press.
Lomnitz-Adler, Claudio. 1991. "Concepts for the Study of Regional Culture." *American Ethnologist* 18:195–214.
Long, Norman. 1973. "The Role of Regional Associations in Peru." In *The Process of Urbanization*, 173–88. Bletch, Buckinghamshire: The Open University.
Long, Norman, and Bryan R. Roberts, eds. 1978. *Peasant Cooperation and Capitalist Expansion in Central Peru*. Austin: Institute of Latin American Studies and the University of Texas Press.
———. 1984. *Miners, Peasants and Entrepreneurs: Regional Development in the Central Highlands of Peru*. New York: Cambridge University Press.
Lovoll, Odd Sverre. 1975. *A Folk Epic: The Bygdelag in America*. Boston: Twayne Publishers.
Mangin, William. 1959. "The Role of Voluntary Associations in the Adaptation of the Rural Population in Peru." *Sociologus* 9:23–35.
———. 1973. "Sociological, Cultural, and Political Characteristics of Some Urban Migrants in Peru. In Aidan Southall, ed., *Urban Anthropology: Cross-Cultural Studies of Urbanization*, 315–50. New York: Oxford University Press.
———. 1970a. "Similarities and Differences Between Two Types of Peruvian Communities." In William Mangin, ed., *Peasants in Cities: Readings in the Anthropology of Urbanization*, 20–29. Boston: Houghton Mifflin.
———. 1970b. "Urbanization Case History in Peru." In William Mangin, ed., *Peasants in Cities: Readings in the Anthropology of Urbanization*, 47–54. Boston: Houghton Mifflin.
Marroquín Zaleta, Enrique. 1987. "Presencia protestante en las comunidades indígenas de Oaxaca." In *De sectas a sectas: Una aproximación al estudio de un fenómeno apasionante*, 35–46. Oaxaca: Universidad Autónoma "Benito Juárez" de Oaxaca and the Claves Latinoamericanas/Instituto de Investigaciones Sociológicas, Mexico City.
———. 1989. "El campo religioso en las comunidades indígenas de Oaxaca." *Cristianismo y Sociedad* 27 (3): 59–71.
Martínez Luna, Jaime. 1982. "Resistencia comunitaria y cultura popular: El caso de la 'Organización en Defensa de los Recursos Naturales y el Desarrollo Social de la Sierra Juárez, A.C.' " In Guillermo Bonfil Batalla, ed. *Culturas populares, Política cultural*, 65–78. Mexico City: Museo de Culturas Populares and the Secretaría de Educación Pública.
Meillassoux, Claude. 1981. *Maidens, Meal and Money: Capitalism and the Domestic Economy*. New York: Cambridge University Press.
Mejía Piñeros, María Consuelo, and Sergio Sarmiento Silva. 1987. *La lucha indígena: Un retrato de la ortodoxia*. Mexico City: Siglo Veintiuno Editores.
Mendez y Mercado, Leticia Irene. 1985. *Migración: Decisión involuntaria*. Mexico City: Instituto Nacional Indigenista.

Mitchell, J. Clyde. 1987. *Cities, Society, and Social Perception*. Oxford: Clarendon Press.

Miyabara, Yasuharu. 1988. *Hokorite Ari: "Kensei Gijuku" Amerika e Wataru*. Tokyo: Kodansha.

Muñoz, Humberto, Orlandina de Oliveira, and Claudio Stern. 1977. *Migración y desigualdad social en la ciudad de México*. Mexico City: Instituto de Investigaciones Sociales, Universidad Nacional Autónoma de México.

Muntzel, Martha C., and Benjamín Pérez González. 1987. "Panorama general de las lenguas indígenas." *América Indígena* 47:571–605.

Murphy, Arthur D., and Alex Stepick. 1991. *Social Inequality in Oaxaca: A History of Resistance and Change*. Philadelphia: Temple University Press.

Myrdal, Gunnar. 1969. *Objectivity in Social Research*. New York: Pantheon.

Nader, Laura. 1964. *Talea and Juquila: A Comparison of Zapotec Social Organization*. Berkeley: University of California Press.

———. 1969. "The Zapotec of Oaxaca." In Robert Wauchope and Evon Z. Vogt, eds., *Handbook of Middle American Indians*, 7:329–59. Austin: University of Texas Press.

———. 1977. "Perspectives Gained From Fieldwork." In Sol Tax and Leslie G. Freeman, eds., *Horizons of Anthropology*, 2d ed., 187–98. Chicago: Aldine.

———. 1989. "The Crown, the Colonists, and the Course of Zapotec Village Law." In June Starr and Jane F. Collier, eds., *History and Power in the Study of Law: New Directions in Legal Anthropology*, 320–44. Ithaca, N.Y.: Cornell University Press.

———. 1990. *Harmony Ideology: Justice and Control in a Zapotec Mountain Village*. Stanford, Calif.: Stanford University Press.

Nagengast, Carole, and Michael Kearney. 1990. "Mixtec Ethnicity: Social Identity, Political Consciousness, and Political Activism." *Latin American Research Review* 25:61–91.

Nolasco Armas, Margarita. 1972. *Oaxaca indígena (Problemas de aculturación en el Estado de Oaxaca y subáreas culturales)*. Instituto de Investigación e Integración Social del Estado de Oaxaca, Investigaciones series, no. 1. Mexico City: Secretaría de Educación Pública.

———. 1985. *Café y sociedad en México*. Mexico City: Centro de Ecodesarrollo.

Nolasco Armas, Margarita, ed. 1979. *Migración municipal en México (1960–1970)*. Vol. 1. Mexico City: Instituto Nacional de Antropología e Historia.

Okamura, Jonathan Y. 1982. "Filipino Hometown Associations in Hawaii." *Ethnology* 22:341–53.

Oliveira, Orlandina de. 1976. *Migración y absorción de mano de obra en la ciudad de México, 1930–1970*. Cuardernos del CES. Mexico City: Centro de Estudios Sociológicos, el Colegio de México.

Oliveira, Orlandina de, and Claudio Stern. 1974. "Notas acerca de la teoría de las migraciones: Aspectos sociológicos." In *Las Migraciones internas en América Latina*, 59–82. Buenos Aires: Ediciones Nueva Visión.

Orellana S., Carlos L. 1973. "Mixtec Migrants in Mexico City: A Case Study of Urbanization." *Human Organization* 32:273–83.

Palmer, Robin. 1991. "Migration, Incapsulation and Ethnicity: Italian Villagers in

London." In A. D. Spiegel and P. A. McAllister, eds., *Tradition and Transition in Southern Africa*, 87–102. Johannesburg: Witwatersrand University Press.

Parnell, Philip C. 1988. *Escalating Disputes: Social Participation and Change in the Oaxacan Highlands*. Tucson: University of Arizona Press.

Partridge, William L., Antoinette B. Brown, and Jeffrey B. Nugent. 1982. "The Papaloapan Dam and Resettlement Project: Human Ecology and Health Impacts." In Art Hansen and Anthony Oliver-Smith, eds., *Involuntary Migration and Resettlement: The Problems and Responses of Dislocated People*, 245–63. Boulder, Colo.: Westview Press.

Pelto, Pertti, and Gretal H. Pelto. 1978. *Anthropological Research: The Structure of Inquiry*. 2d ed. New York: Cambridge University Press.

Pérez García, Rosendo. 1956. *La Sierra Juárez*. Vols. 1–2. Mexico City: Gráfica Cervantina.

Perlman, Janice E. 1974. *Methodological Notes on Complex Survey Research Involving Life History Data*. Institute of Urban and Regional Development, Monograph no. 18. Berkeley: University of California.

——. 1976. *The Myth of Marginality: Urban Poverty and Politics in Rio de Janeiro*. Berkeley: University of California Press.

Pickvance, C. G. 1986. "Voluntary Associations." In Robert G. Burgess, ed., *Key Variables in Social Investigation*, 223–45. London: Routledge and Kegan Paul.

Pitt-Rivers, Julian. 1961. *People of the Sierra*. Chicago: University of Chicago Press.

Poleman, Thomas T. 1964. *The Papaloapan Project: Agricultural Development in the Mexican Tropics*. Stanford, Calif.: Stanford University Press.

Pozas, Ricardo, and Isabel H. de Pozas. 1977. *Los Indios en las clases sociales de México*. 6th ed. Mexico City: Siglo Veintiuno.

Price, Charles A. 1963. *Southern Europeans in Australia*. Melbourne: Oxford University Press.

Rex, John, Daniele Joly, and Czarina Wilpert, eds. 1987. *Immigrant Associations in Europe*. Aldershot, Eng.: Gower Publishing Company.

Reyes Ruiz, Ignacio. 1981. "Relato de un Zapoteco en proceso de aculturación." *Revista Mexicana de Ciencias Políticas y Sociales* 27:121–26.

Roberts, Bryan R. 1974. "The Interrelationships of City and Provinces in Peru and Guatemala." *Latin American Urban Research* 4:207–35.

——. 1981. "Migration and Industrializing Economies: A Comparative Perspective." In Jorge Balán, ed., *Why People Move: Comparative Perspectives on the Dynamics of Internal Migration*, 17–42. Paris: UNESCO.

——. 1990. "The Informal Sector in Comparative Perspective." In M. Estellie Smith, ed., *Perspectives on the Informal Economy*, 23–48. Monographs on Economic Anthropology, No. 8. Lanham, Md.: University Press of America.

Rollwagen, Jack. 1974. "Mediation and Rural–Urban Migration in Mexico: A Proposal and a Case Study." *Latin American Urban Research* 4:47–63.

Romer, Marta. 1982. *Comunidad, migración y desarrollo: El Caso de los Mixes de Totontepec*. Mexico City: Instituto National Indigenista.

Romero Frizzi, María de los Angeles. 1988. "La antropología en Oaxaca." In Carlos García Mora, ed., *La antropología en México: Panorama histórico*, vol. 15: *La antropología en el sur de México,* 181–203. Mexico City: Instituto Nacional de Antropología e Historia.

Royce, Ana Peterson. 1975. *Prestigio y afiliación en una comunidad urbana: Juchitán, Oaxaca.* Mexico City: Instituto Nacional Indigenista.

Sanjek, Roger, ed. 1990. *Fieldnotes: The Makings of Anthropology.* Ithaca, N.Y.: Cornell University Press.

Schteingart, Martha. 1988. "Mexico City." In Mattei Dogan and John D. Kasarda, eds., *The Metropolis Era,* vol. 2: *Mega Cities,* 268–93. Newbury Park, Calif.: Sage.

Selby, Henry A. 1974. *Zapotec Deviance: The Convergence of Folk and Modern Sociology.* Austin: University of Texas Press.

Simpson, Lesley Byrd. 1971. *Many Mexicos.* Berkeley: University of California Press.

Singer, Paul. 1977. *Economía política de la urbanización.* 2d ed. Mexico City: Siglo Veintiuno.

Slater, David. 1989. *Territory and State Power in Latin America: The Peruvian Case.* New York: St. Martin's Press.

Stavenhagen, Rodolfo. 1976. "Capitalismo y campesinado en México." In *Capitalismo y campesinado en México: Estudios de la realidad campesina,* 11–27. Mexico City: Instituto Nacional de Antropología e Historia.

———. 1986a. "La cultura popular y la creación intelectual." *La palabra y el hombre* 57:5–18.

———. 1986b "Culture and Society in Latin America: A Reappraisal." *Ethnic Studies Report* 4:50–58.

———. 1989. "Comunidades étnicas en estados modernos." *América Indígena* 49:11–34.

Stephen, Lynne. 1991. *Zapotec Women.* Austin: University of Texas Press.

Stern, Claudio. 1982. "Industrialisation and Migration in Mexico." In Peter Peek and Guy Standing, eds., *State Policies and Migration: Studies in Latin America and the Caribbean,* 173–205. London: Croom Helm.

Sutton, Susan Buck. 1978. Migrant Regional Associations: An Athenian Example and Its Implications. Ph.D. diss., University of North Carolina.

———. 1983. Migrant Associations and Regional Disparities. Paper presented at the 1983 Meeting of the Society for Applied Anthropology, San Diego, California, 17–19 March.

Unikel, Luis. 1971. "The Process of Urbanization in Mexico: Distribution and Growth of Urban Population." *Latin American Urban Research* 1:247–302.

Unikel, Luis, Crescensio Ruiz Chiapetto, and Gustavo Garza Villarreal. 1976. *El desarrollo urbano de México: Diagnóstico e implicaciones futuras.* Mexico City: Colegio de México.

Varese, Stefano. 1983. *Indígenas y educación en México.* Mexico City: Centro de Estudios Educativos.

———. 1985. "Cultural Development in Ethnic Groups: Anthropological Explorations in Education." *International Social Science Journal* (New York: UNESCO) 37, no. 2 (issue 104): 201–16.

Vélez-Ibañez, Carlos G. 1988. "Networks of Exchange Among Mexicans in the U.S.

and Mexico: Local Level Mediating Responses to National and International Transformations." *Urban Anthropology* 17:27–51.
Walton, John. 1982. "The International Economy and Peripheral Urbanism." In Norman I. Fainstein and Susan S. Fainstein, eds., *Urban Policy Under Capitalism*, 119–35. Beverly Hills: Sage.
Weaver, Thomas, and Theodore E. Downing, eds. 1976. *Mexican Migration*. Tucson: Bureau of Ethnic Research, Department of Anthropology, University of Arizona.
Weisser, Michael R. 1985. *A Brotherhood of Memory: Jewish Landsmanshaftn in the New World*. New York: Basic Books.
Whitecotton, Joseph W. 1977. *The Zapotecs: Princes, Priests, and Peasants*. Norman: University of Oklahoma Press.
Whiting, Beatriz Blyth. 1950. *Paiute Sorcery*. New York: Viking Fund.
Williams, Thomas Rhys. 1967. *Field Methods in the Study of Culture*. New York: Holt, Rinehart and Winston.
Wolf, Eric. 1959. *Sons of the Shaking Earth*. Chicago: University of Chicago Press.
———. 1967. "Levels of Communal Relations." In Manning Nash, ed., *Handbook of Middle American Indians*, 6:299–316. Austin: University of Texas Press.
Young, C. M. 1976. The Social Setting of Migration: Factors Affecting Migration from a Sierra Zapotec Village in Oaxaca, Mexico. Ph.D. diss., University of London.
Young, Kate. 1978a. "Modes of Appropriation and the Sexual Division of Labour." In Annette Kuhn and AnnMarie Wolpe, eds., *Feminism and Materialism*, 124–54. Boston: Routledge and Kegan Paul.
———. 1978b. "Economía campesina, unidad doméstica y migración." *América Indígena* 38:279–302.
———. 1982. "The Creation of a Relative Surplus Population: A Case Study From Mexico." In Lourdes Benería, ed., *Women and Development: The Sexual Division of Labor in Rural Societies*, 149–77. New York: Praeger.
Zabin, Carol, coordinator. 1992. *Migración oaxaqueña a los campos agrícolas de California: Un diálogo*. Current Issue Brief No. 2. San Diego: Center for U.S.–Mexican Studies, University of California, San Diego.

INDEX

Administration: regional, 31, 58–60
Agriculture, 28, 31, 58, 139n.4; Lahoyan, 43–45, 137n.3; modernization of, 29, 42; Ralu'an, 50–52, 57, 69, 71; in sierra, 32, 61–62, 80
Alemán, Miguel, 31, 56
Altamirano, Teófilo, 20–23, 135nn.7, 13, 140n.3
Assimilation, 30, 120, 129
Associations, 5, 18, 47, 54, 127; definition and development of, 14–15, 20; migrant, 3–4, 8–9, 14–15, 97; regional, 17, 102–4, 115–16, 117–18, 120, 125–26, 129–30, 135nn.8, 9; role of, 21–23, 115; social psychology of, 15–16; village, 89–93, 119, 121–22, 126
Authority, 79–80

Bakeries: in Oaxaca City, 82–83
Bands, 46–47, 49, 138n.9
Bataillon, Claude, 17
Beals, Ralph, 30
Bourdieu, Pierre, 9, 127–28, 140n.4
Bracero program, 28, 32, 64, 69–70, 76, 79
Bravo, Sra., 64

Caleros, 59–60, 105–6
Cancian, Francesca M., 113, 128
Capital: cultural, 3, 9, 127–28, 133n.1, 140n.4
Capitalism, 20, 33
Cárdenas, Lázaro, 30
Cargo system, 49, 106
Catholicism, 47–48, 61
Class, 22–23, 116–17. *See also* Status
Coffee production, 28, 31, 48, 51, 69, 71, 138n.10
Colonial period, 13–14, 27–28

Comisión de Luz, 90
Comisión de Papaloapan. *See* Papaloapan Commission
Comité Villalteco, 105
Communities, 118, 123–24; common values of, 112–13, 127–28; labor for, 113–14; Oaxacan, 32–33; Zapotec, 28–29
Compadrazgo, 95, 97
Competition for resources, 16–17, 19
Comunicaciones Vecinales, 56
CONASUPO, 57
Confederación de Trabajadores Mexicanos (CTM), 116
Conflict, 66–67. *See also* Factionalism
Cooperation, 3, 7, 19, 36, 127–28
Copa Bitoo, 114
Credentialism, 34
Critical mass, 114, 140n.2
Cruz, Sr., 94
CTM. *See* Confederación de Trabajadores Mexicanos
Culture, 133n.1, 134n.2

Departamento de Caminos Vecinales, 91
Department of Commerce and Public Works, 56
Department of Communications, 89–90
Department of Local Communications, 56
Department of Local Roads, 91
Depression, 69
Development, 3, 9, 19, 57, 92, 106, 126; in home community, 18, 116; in Lahoya, 42–43, 48–49, 89–92; and Mexico City, 33–34; and migrant associations, 23, 121; regional, 29, 103, 118; rural, 60–61, 126, 129
Discrimination, 83–84, 94
Domínguez, Sr., 83

153

Economy, 4, 36, 127, 137n.2; Lahoyan, 43–45, 61–62, 119; Ralu'an, 50–52; Villaltecan, 58–59, 62
Education, 29, 31, 34, 36, 61, 88; migration for, 64, 66, 67, 70, 71, 73, 74–75, 76, 86–87, 125; and treatment, 83–84
Electrification, 57, 90
Elites, 70, 75, 79, 115, 116, 121, 124
Employment, 18, 48, 114, 137n.14; in Mexico City, 33, 71, 76, 84–86, 96, 97, 105, 107, 125; and migrant associations, 115–16; in Oaxaca City, 82–84, 94, 95, 124
Endogamy, 29, 46, 53–54, 114
Escuela Tecnológica Agropecuaria, 100
Ethnicity, 4, 13, 134n.4
Ethnography, 35

Facilitation, 82, 84, 95–96, 98, 104
Factionalism, 60; in Lahoya, 65, 67, 78; migrant, 5, 7, 90–93, 121, 139–40n.6
Families, 46; and authority, 79–80; conflicts in, 66–67, 68–69, 78; in Mexico City, 87, 95; migration of, 72, 77; Ralu'an, 52–54, 70, 76; wealthy, 52–53
Fernández, Don, 85
Fieldwork, 35–40, 136n.7, 137n.12
Fiestas, 106
Formal sector, 137n.14
Foster, George M., xiii, 12, 112, 129
Friendship, 95, 97
Fuente, Julio de la, 102, 118
Fund raising, 56, 100–102

Gamio, Manuel, 29–30
González, Sr., 85–86, 87
Gozona, 36, 47, 54, 128, 138n.13
Grupo Progreso, 88
Guatemala City, 19–20

Health, 31, 136n.3
Health centers, 99–100, 102–3
Hernández, Fidencio, 55
Hidalgo (Lahoya), 46
Historical structuralism, 8; perspectives on migrant associations, 19–21, 22–23, 32
Housing, 18, 97, 114, 116

Identity, 4, 16, 113, 118; with home village, 11–12; regional, 12–14, 114
Import substitution, 32
Imprisonment, 87–88

Income, 45, 62, 97
Indians: integration of, 29–30
Indigenista movement, 30
INMECAFE, 28, 57
Industrialization, 8, 19, 20, 32, 96
Industry, 33, 34
Informal sector, 38
Infrastructure: Lahoyan, 89–93, 119; in Sierra Juárez, 28, 31
INI. *See* Instituto Nacional Indigenista
INMECAFE, 28, 57
Instituto Nacional Indigenista (INI), 30
Integration, 118; social, 21–22, 29–30, 32
Ixtlán, 48

Jiménez, Sr., 73
Jobs. *See* Employment
Jongkind, Fred, 18, 22, 115
José, Sra., 68
Juárez, Benito, 13
Juárez (Lahoya), 46
Juquila, 42

Kearney, Michael, 49, 129, 130, 133n.2, 136n.8
Kinship, 20, 82, 95, 97, 112

Labor, 61–62, 69, 138n.12; communal, 113–14; unpaid, 36, 71, 89, 90, 91, 93, 99; unskilled, 34, 35, 38; wage, 44–45, 48, 51, 52, 53, 54
Lachatao, 42
Lachirioag, 114
Ladinos, 19, 20
Lahoya, 29, 60, 117, 123, 126, 129, 133n.3, 138n.9, 139n.1; agriculture in, 43–45, 137n.3; conservatism of, 49–50; development in, 42–43, 48–49, 116, 121; divisions in, 46–47; economy in, 43–45, 61–62; factionalism in, 65, 67, 90–92, 139–40n.6; families in, 46; government in, 45–46; improvement projects for, 89–93; migrants from, 5, 7, 38–39, 75, 82–89, 107, 114, 118–19, 124–25; out-migration from, 63–69, 81; population of, 41–42, 77; poverty in, 77–78; religion in, 47–48, 61; social organization of, 46–47
Lahoyan Development Association, 89
Land, 44, 46, 53, 63, 69, 71, 78
Language barrier, 64–67, 76, 83–84, 87
Land reform, 29, 31

Leisure activities, 15, 93–94
Lighting Commission, 90
Lima, 16, 18, 19, 20–21
Liquor, 51–52, 138 n. 7
Literacy, 29, 61
Long, Norman, 19, 20, 62, 135 n. 12
Los Angeles, 114

Maids, from Lahoya, 65, 66, 68–69, 75, 81, 83, 86–88
Mangin, William, 16
Mantaro Valley, 20, 21
Market centers, 43, 44, 50, 58, 59, 117, 123–24
Marriage, 46, 53–54, 114
Martínez, Señorita, 65–66, 68–69
Mayordomía, 47, 48, 59, 106
Men: migration by, 64, 67, 75, 81, 82–83, 84
Mendiolea, David, 59, 74, 106, 121
Mestizos, 13, 29–30, 58
Mexican Revolution, 28, 29–30, 31, 69
Mexico City, 4, 5, 33, 34, 111, 136 n. 6; employment in, 76, 96, 114; Lahoyans in, 84–89; migration to, 33–35, 65–68, 71–73, 81, 83, 107, 125; Ralu'ans in, 37–38, 95; regional associations in, 102–4; village associations in, 89–92; Villaltecos in, 105–7
Migrants: characteristics of, 81, 139 n. 2; Lahoyan, 5, 7, 38–39, 75, 82–89, 93–94; Ralu'an, 94–105
Migration, 4, 8, 19, 33; chain, 5, 72, 111, 114, 125; from Lahoya, 63–69; to Mexico City, 33–35; patterns of, 36, 80–81; from Ralu'a, 69–74; stated motives for, 75–76, 77–81, 124, 139 n. 6; from Villa Alta, 60, 74–75, 76–77
Mining industry, 48
Mixe, 115
Mixtecs, 18, 115
Mobility, 36, 139 n. 6
Modernization, 8, 29–30, 32, 36, 42, 118, 135–36 n. 2
Modernization theory, 15
Municipalities, 5, 29, 45–46
Mutual aid, 3, 7, 17, 19, 82, 117, 123, 126–27, 135 n. 10; and employment, 85–86, 96–97; and language barriers, 87–88; and migrant associations, 14, 18; Ralu'an, 54, 98–102, 104–5, 119–20;

and standards of living, 96–97. *See also* Gozona; Tequio

Nader, Laura, xiii, 32, 35–36, 54–55, 133 n. 2, 137 n. 4, 138 n. 8
Nationalism, 29
Natividad, 42
Neighborhoods, 88
Networks, 22, 88, 97, 104, 112; informal, 18, 115; reciprocity, 7, 133 n. 3; social, 97–98
Nexitzo, 13, 133 n. 3
Norms, 11, 72, 113, 128, 134 n. 2

OAS, 30
Oaxaca, 6 (fig.), 27–28
Oaxaca de Juárez (Oaxaca City), 5, 27, 70; Caleros in, 105–6; employment in, 82–84, 94, 95; migration to, 64–65, 66, 74, 75; road construction to, 55–57
Orellana S., Carlos, 17–18, 135 n. 71
Out-migration. *See* Migration

Pacification, 41
Paisanazgo, 3, 8, 9, 13–14, 72, 82, 107; bases of, in Mexico City, 111–13; conditions framing appearance of, 113–14; as cultural capital, 3, 9, 122, 127–28, 133 n. 1; for Ralu'ans, 95–96
Paisanos, xi, 8, 10–11, 104–5, 111–12, 134 n. 1
Panela production, 42, 43
Papaloapan Commission, 31–32, 56, 99, 100
Papelería de Tuxtepec, 99
Parnell, Philip C., 7, 39, 59–60, 105, 106, 107, 129
Patria chica, 12
Patronage, 121, 126
Pepper production, 31
Perlman, Janice, 36, 137 n. 11
Peru, 20
Pineda, Sr., 74
Political bosses, 59–60
Political organization, 62
Political rights, 29
Politics: Villa Alta, 59, 105–6, 120–22; workplace, 103–4, 121
Politicization, 126
Poverty, 70–71, 77–78
Prejudice, 83–84
Priests, 79

Professor, the, 88, 89, 90, 91–92, 119, 126, 139 n. 1
Progressives, 105
Protestants, 61, 120
Pueblismo, 8, 10, 11–12, 14, 129; labor and, 113–14; among Zapotecs, 114–15

Race, 13
Ralu'a, 11, 29, 32, 43, 48, 123–24, 133 n. 3, 138 n. 12; agriculture in, 50–51; development of, 57, 60–61, 116, 121; economy of, 51–52, 57–58, 61–62; families in, 53–54; fieldwork in, 36–37, 137 n. 13; improvement projects in, 99–102; migrants from, 7, 12–13, 37–38, 75–76, 78–79, 94–105, 107, 111–12, 114, 117–18, 119–20, 125–26, 134–35 n. 5, 138 n. 14; out-migration from, 69–74, 78, 81; population of, 50, 77; poverty in, 70–71, 77; road construction to, 55–57; social organization of, 54–55; social stratification in, 52–53
Ramírez, Sr., 73
Reciprocity, 7, 133 n. 3
Regionalism, 4, 5. *See also* Pueblismo; Paisanazgo
Regional Zapotec Association, 102–3, 120, 139–40 n. 6
Religion, 47–48, 49, 61
República de los Indios, La, 28
Resources: competition for, 16–17, 19
Reyes, Sra., 83
Rincón, 12–13, 29, 32, 102, 127–28, 133 n. 3
Rinconeros, 12–13
Roads, 69, 139 n. 2; Lahoya-Ralu'a, 48–49, 53, 90, 91–93; Ralu'a-Oaxaca City, 55–57, 99; Villa Alta, 59, 106
Roberts, Bryan, 17, 19, 20, 62
Rodríguez, Sra., 86–87
Rollwagen, Jack, 126
Romer, Marta, 22, 115
Ruiz Cortines, President, 31, 90
Rural areas, 8, 19, 31, 34–35

Salazar, Sr., 85
San Ildefonso Villa Alta. *See* Villa Alta
San Juan Juquila Vijanos, 13, 45
San Miguel Cajonos, 44
San Miguel del Río, 42

Santo Entierro fiesta, 106
Scholars, 66, 70, 73, 79, 124
Schools, 30, 31, 99, 100
Secretariat of Public Works, 100
Sierra Juárez, 3, 5, 29, 31, 32, 80–81
Social organization: in Lahoya, 46–47; of migrants, 5, 36, 88–89, 97, 117; Ralu'an, 54–55
Social stratification, 11–12, 19–20, 46, 52–53
Sociopsychology of migrant associations, 15–16
Solaga, 43
Solidarity, 4, 11
Soyaltepec, 18, 135 n. 11
Spain: colonial administration of, 27–28, 41, 50, 58; rural culture of, 12, 129
Standards of living, 70, 96–97
Status, 22, 34. *See also* Class; Social stratification
Structuralism. *See* Historical structuralism
Sugarcane production, 31, 42, 43

Tamayo, José L., 55, 56
Tanetze, 13, 42
Taxation, 31
Teachers, 32, 48, 70, 74–75, 88
Telegraph, 31, 57, 75, 105, 106
Telephone service, 89–90
Tequio, 36, 71, 89, 91, 128, 137 n. 4; for road construction, 56, 90, 99
Tertiary sector, 33
Torre, Sr., 67
Totontepec, 115
Transportation, 69, 80; and road construction, 55–57, 139 n. 2. *See also* Roads

UNESCO, 30
Union of Zapotec Villages, 103–4, 115–16
Unions, 97, 114, 120, 126
United States, 28, 64, 69–70
Urban areas, 14, 16, 18, 19–20, 128–29. *See also* Oaxaca de Juárez; Mexico City

Values, 112–13, 127–28, 134 n. 2
Vasconcelos, Eduardo, 55
Velásquez, Fidel, 104
Villa Alta, 4–5, 6 (fig.), 7, 13, 29, 33, 62, 116, 117, 123, 125; administration from, 31, 58–60; economy of, 61–62; out-

migration from, 76–77, 81; politics of, 58–60, 120–22; population of, 58, 60, 77. *See also* Villaltecos
Villalteco Cultural Association, 105–6
Villaltecos, 7–8, 58, 138n.15; in Mexico City, 39, 105–7; political issues of, 120–21; as teachers, 74–75, 77
Voluntary associations, definition of, 14

Witchcraft, 49, 62, 138n.8
Women, 64, 88, 98; in Mexico City, 65–66, 67, 84, 86–87; migration by, 75, 81, 83
World War II, 28

Yalalag, 43, 59

Zacatepec, 60
Zapotecs, 4–5, 114–15
Zoogocho, 11, 43, 44, 114

ABOUT THE AUTHOR

Lane Ryo Hirabayashi received his Ph.D. in anthropology from the University of California at Berkeley in 1981. His areas of interest include ethnicity, urban anthropology, kinship and social organization, and the anthropology of Mexico and Latin America. Between 1984 and 1990, Hirabayashi was Associate and then Full Professor at the School of Ethnic Studies at San Francisco State University. In 1991 he joined the Department of Anthropology at the University of Colorado at Boulder as an Associate Professor and became a core faculty member of the Center for Studies of Ethnicity and Race in America (CSERA). Hirabayashi has published articles on Rincón Zapotec migrants in *Urban Anthropology, América Indígena,* and the *Latin American Research Review,* and he is a co-editor with the Peruvian anthropologist Teófilo Altamirano of *Migrants, Regional Cultures and Latin American Cities.* He is currently working on a manuscript on a Japanese American community and the politics of a southern California city.